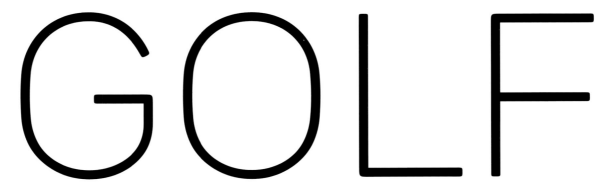

GOLF

The Iconic Courses

Quarto

First published in 2025 by Ivy Press
an imprint of The Quarto Group.
One Triptych Place, London, SE1 9SH
United Kingdom
T (0)20 7700 9000
www.Quarto.com

EEA Representation, WTS Tax d.o.o., Žanova ulica 3, 4000
Kranj, Slovenia

A catalogue record for this book is available from
the British Library.

ISBN 978-071129-850-7
EBook ISBN 978-07112-9851-4

10 9 8 7 6 5 4 3 2 1

Design concept by Glenn Howard
Design by Cara Rogers
Senior Designer Renata Latipova
Publisher Richard Green
Production Controller Rohanna Yusof and Alex Merrett

Printed in China

Picture Credits
Getty Images (David Cannon): Pages 4,16,17,18, 19, 21, 26, 27,
28/29, 30, 31, 32, 33, 34/35, 36-37, 38, 39, 42/43, 44, 45, 49,
52/53, 54, 55, 58, 59 (top), 60, 61, 62/63, 64 (bottom), 65, 66/67,
68, 69, 74-75, 76 (top), 77,78, 79 (top), 80/81, 82, 83, 84, 85,
87, 89 (bottom), 90, 91 (top), 100/101, 102, 103, 104/105, 106,
107, 114, 116/117, 118, 119, 124/125, 126, 127, 132/133, 134,
135, 136/137, 138, 139, 140/141, 142, 143 (top), 146/147, 148,
149, 150, 151, 152/153, 156, 157, 166, 167, 172/173, 174/175,
176/177, 178, 179, 180, 181, 182/183, 184, 185, 186-187,188,
189, 190, 191, 192, 193, 194, 195, 202, 203.
Getty Images: Pages 56/57, 59 (bottom), 64 (top), 76 (bottom), 86,
91 (bottom), 92/93, 96 (top), 97, 98, 99, 115, 122, 123, 143 (bottom), 144 (top), 145, 164, 165, 168-169, 212, 213.
Gary Lisbon: Pages 6/7, 10/11, 12, 13, 14, 15, 20, 22/23, 24, 25,
46/47, 48, 51, 94/95, 96 (bottom), 110/111, 112, 113, 120/121,
130/131, 144 (bottom), 160, 161, 162/163, 198, 199, 200, 201,
204/205, 206, 207, 208/209, 210, 211, 216, 217, 218/219, 220,
221, 222, 223, 224, 225, 226/227, 228, 229, 230, 231, 232/233,
234, 235, 236, 237, 238, 239.
Shutterstock: Pages 40/41, 72/73. 88, 89 (top), 159.
Lehavre-etretat-tourisme.com: Page 158.

Page 4 **The Royal West Norfolk links near
Brancaster in England. One of the few golf
courses where players can get cut off by the tide.**

GOLF

The Iconic Courses

Frank Hopkinson

IVY PRESS

CONTENTS

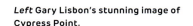

INTRODUCTION

For the player in pursuit of the greatest golfing experience, there has never been a better time to be alive. The great old courses will always be with us, the monuments of the game that from time to get a little spit and polish, a rebuilt green here, a new tee there. Then there are the new courses, more often than not at the high end of the green fee table. Bandon Dunes in Oregon has many great courses but the recent Sheep Farm has eclipsed them all. In New Zealand, the teams of Coore & Crenshaw and Tom Doak have created two outstanding new courses at Te Ārai which have bolstered the country's reputation as home to the finest golf courses.

On the other side of the world there is the Ardfin Estate on the southern tip of Jura in the Inner Hebrides. Those with the golfing gene, the author included, will have seen stretches of coastline and immediately conjured up the thought of a golf course there. At Ardfin this is exactly what the owner has done amidst some of the greatest scenery Scotland has to offer. Further north, at Durness, close to Cape Wrath, there is a pioneering nine-hole course built by keen local enthusiasts, the way golf started out. There is no 'well-stocked pro's shop' or 'fabulous practice range', just nine holes laid out by the members looking down on the quiet splendour of Balnakiel Bay and for the slimmest of charges.

This book celebrates them all. It is not a collection of the best golf courses or the most beautiful courses, though many of the inclusions would tick both boxes. It is a gathering together of some of the world's most distinctive courses. For this endeavour I have leaned heavily on the work of two of the world's greatest golf photographers, David Cannon of Getty Images and Gary Lisbon. It is thanks to their extraordinary output that it has been possible to convey the awe and wonder golfers often feel walking upon the hallowed ground of the great fairway turf.

There is a category of art known as 'Land Art' where artists use shapes and forms from the natural environment to create works of art. With many new courses, golfers get to play a work of art.

Given the global reach of golf, it will be fascinating to see where striking new courses will be added to the inventory of future venues. Nick Faldo's remarkable course at Laguna Lăng Cô in Vietnam may be indicative of the direction of travel, but there are also bold ventures in Scotland, in Iceland and the success of the Lofoten Links in Norway may prompt further Scandinavian expansion. We can be reassured that there are many more iconic courses to come.

Frank Hopkinson

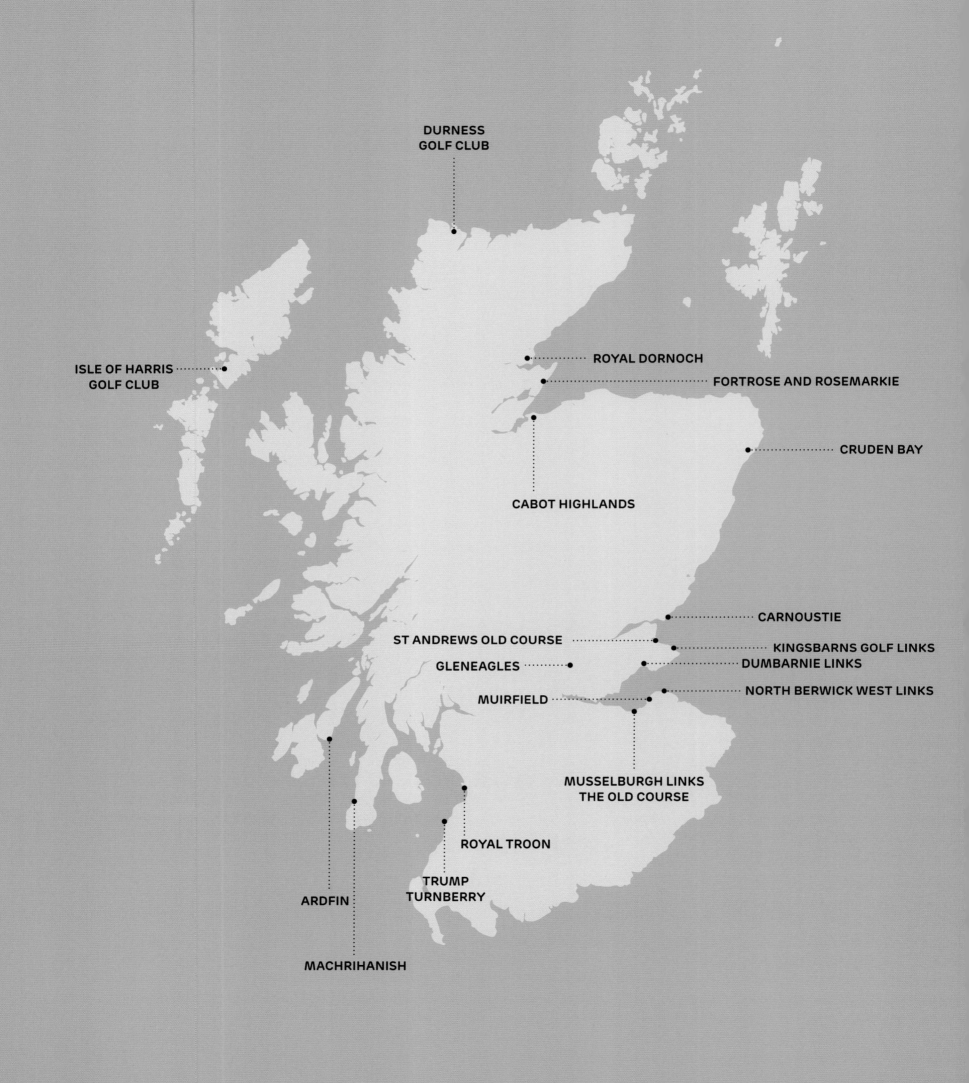

DURNESS
GOLF CLUB

ISLE OF HARRIS
GOLF CLUB

ROYAL DORNOCH

FORTROSE AND ROSEMARKIE

CRUDEN BAY

CABOT HIGHLANDS

CARNOUSTIE

ST ANDREWS OLD COURSE

KINGSBARNS GOLF LINKS

GLENEAGLES

DUMBARNIE LINKS

MUIRFIELD

NORTH BERWICK WEST LINKS

MUSSELBURGH LINKS
THE OLD COURSE

ROYAL TROON

ARDFIN

TRUMP
TURNBERRY

MACHRIHANISH

SCOTLAND

BOB HARRISON HAS DESIGNED A COURSE THAT LEAVES GOLF WRITERS STRUGGLING FOR NEW SUPERLATIVES

ARDFIN ESTATE

THE LONG ROAD, ISLE OF JURA, SCOTLAND

Ardfin is as close as you'll get to a fantasy golf course. While many amateur golfers dream of winning big on the lottery and creating their own golf course, retired Australian hedge fund manager Greg Coffey made it a reality when he bought the 11,500-acre Ardfin Estate in Scotland.

There is a snag, though.

Ardfin is on the southern shores of Jura, one of the largest islands of the Inner Hebrides. There is no stumbling upon it, serious travel plans must be made to get there. Added to that, it is a very exclusive venue. When it opened in 2015 it was restricted to Coffey's family, friends and business associates — the rest of the envious golfing world looked on.

Then, in 2020, it was opened up to the public with the proviso that two nights' accommodation on the estate's various high-end properties must be booked as part of the visit. If this is added to the cost of the golf it is likely to exceed the annual membership fees for most top clubs in the UK. However given its remote position, play the course and you are likely to be on first name terms with everyone you meet on the course. And that won't be many.

In golfing terms there is nothing to match the sheer unadulterated adventure of a round at Ardfin. Bob Harrison, former lead architect for Greg Norman's design company was given the brief to design the course around the coastline surrounding Jura House. Much of the land was

Above The par-3 10th hole requires a considerable carry from Ardfin's most challenging tee position.

Right From the 11th green it's a short stroll to refreshments in the Boathouse on the shores of the Sound of Islay. It is a great place to linger and with few people on the course, there is little pressure to move on.

Opposite top The 3rd hole takes players to the easterly end of the course. It is a short par-4, but with trouble each side of a narrow fairway accuracy is the key.

Opposite bottom The 8th hole is the first hole to the west of the clubhouse. It's a very short par-4, but long-hitters will have to carry the wall that abuts the small gully.

high on the cliffs, but other parts descended to the water's edge, with one stretch of shoreline that cried out for a drive across water.

The first seven holes head east from Jura House along the top of the cliffs and straight away players realize that there is no need for the unremitting bunkers of a links course when there is so much jeopardy around. This comes on the par-3, 2nd hole in the form of a cliffside chasm demanding players carry to the green, followed by the par-4, 3rd hole which has a similar drive and then a snaking burn to the left as the fairway tumbles downhill.

The 7th hole takes players back to Jura House and then a connecting walk, past the house and an elegant greenhouse with a snack and coffee stop, before tackling the final 11 equally hazardous holes.

As part of the detailed restoration work, the estate's dry-stone walls were rebuilt and one forms a barrier on the short, par-4, 8th discouraging a run-up to the green. Soon it's on to the par-3, 10th which is a headland to headland shot of 183 yards, similar to 'Bruce's Castle' at Turnberry but without the water below. For those running low on their supply of balls there is a closer side tee which doesn't take on the fall to the small ravine. It is an indication of the number of spectacular and well-crafted holes at Ardfin that the 10th is simply one of many distinctive and memorable holes.

Opposite top The shoreside tee and fairway for the beautiful par-4, 13th hole, with authentic bothy and walled stock enclosures.

Opposite bottom On the return home, this is the view from the 15th tee at the westerly end of the course. The boathouse promontory is visible to the right.

Above Looking down onto the 16th green. Below it is the 12th green, the tee for which is to the right of the Boathouse — and if a high sea is running, just in front of the Boathouse. The 11th green is beyond the 12th.

Left A view looking east from above the magnificent Ardfin estate buildings.

The 11th green is down by the boathouse made famous by Scottish band the KLF supposedly burning £1m for art; then it's on to the 12th, a 205-yard, par-3 wallop across the water from a tee right at the water's edge — although mindful of potential wave action in high seas, there is a more substantial one closer inland. The 13th hole, down by the shore, skirts the kind of ruined old farm stockyards that Tom Doak would probably have made central to his Old Petty course at Cabot Highlands, but at Ardfin it's a sideshow to another unique beauty. Then it's on to the 14th before turning uphill for the journey home.

Raised beaches are prominent in Scotland thanks to 'isostatic rebound' where the weight of glaciation has been lifted and the land rises. It's a facet exploited by many of the country's top courses including Ardfin, where the 15th, 16th, 17th and 18th head home on the raised shelf above the current shoreline and the holes below.

Ardfin has been described as a 'modern masterpiece', but given that's a description ascribed to many top-end pay-to-play courses which don't have sumptuous views across the Sound of Islay, that might be selling it short. It's an astonishing bucket list course ... for the small number of people with platinum buckets.

THE COURSE AT CARNOUSTIE TAKES NO PRISONERS, EVEN BEFORE THE WIND STARTS TO BLOW

Opposite The career-wrecking Barry Burn snakes its way across the 17th and 18th fairways of the Championship Course. It also comes into play on the 10th and 11th holes.

Above Carnoustie's 15th hole (Lucky Slap), 16th (Barry Burn), 17th (Island) and pictured above, 18th (Home), are considered four of the scariest closing holes in world golf.

CARNOUSTIE
CARNOUSTIE, ANGUS, SCOTLAND

Golf was played on the dunes crossed by the Barry Burn at Carnoustie as early as 1527, but it was three centuries later that than an official course was laid out. St Andrews' master golfer and ballmaker Allan Robertson brought his apprentice Tom Morris up the coast to help him lay out 10 holes for a course which opened in 1842. Fifteen years later, and after an acrimonious split brought about by Morris's adoption of the gutta percha ball (which threatened Robertson's featherie ball-making business), Morris returned to Carnoustie alone to make it 18 holes in 1857.

Five-time Open Champion James Braid, having turned his golf design skills to create the Kings and Queens courses at Gleneagles, was drafted in to extend and remodel the course in 1926 and the routing of today's course is much as he left it: a brutal and exacting test of golf. The back nine is one of the toughest challenges in championship golf and the closing two holes are crossed and recrossed by the Barry Burn five times.

The Open has returned seven times since Edinburgh golfer Tommy Armour first got his hands on the claret jug in 1931, while Francesco Molinari became the first Italian winner at the most recent Open of 2018. However the indelible memory of Opens played at Carnoustie will always be Frenchman Jean van de Velde's triple-bogey seven on the 18th hole, when all he needed to win was a six.

French sport places an emphasis on winning with *panache*, hence the Tour de France prize for the most heroic move of the day, the *Prix de la combativité*. Van de Velde wanted to end in style, but ended in the Barry Burn. What was not widely understood was that the burn is tidal and was steadily backing up as the tide came in. So when Jean first contemplated a shot from the burn it was a marginal call. A few minutes of world television coverage later, the ball was further submerged and he chose to drop instead.

The Championship Course had been significantly beefed up prior to that 1999 Open, with bunkers being rebuilt, greens enlarged and new tees built extending the length. Amateur golfers tackling this behemoth of difficulty are not rewarded with great vistas, but then again all attention needs to be focused on the task in hand. And when the East wind blows off the North Sea, it is some task.

Above There are nods to the club building at Dinard in the art deco-themed clubhouse gazing out across the Moray Firth.

Opposite Castle Stuart, for which the original course was named, sits beyond the 191-yard, par-3, 4th hole. Castle Stuart hosted the Scottish Open for three successive years from 2011 to 2013, returning again in 2016.

NOT CONTENT WITH CREATING KINGSBARNS, MARK PARSINEN HEADED NORTH TO CARVE OUT ANOTHER CLASSIC ON THE MORAY FIRTH

CABOT HIGHLANDS

INVERNESS, NAIRNSHIRE, SCOTLAND

Having created the Kingsbarns course in Fife, the late Mark Parsinen headed north, to the Highlands and the bonny shores of the Moray Firth. His new project would centre around the Castle Stuart estate, a seventeenth-century tower house along the coast from Inverness that had lain in ruins since the time of Charles I.

This time he employed golf architect Gil Hanse to fulfil his mantra of a course that engaged with the coastline to create an inspiring golfing experience, rather than the Carnoustie format: tough test with sea nearby.

The estuary-fringed land was perfectly suited to the brief, with great views across the short stretch of water to the Black Isle, which is not actually an island, but the peninsula of land between the Moray and Cromarty Firths. Having built Kingsbarns, Parsinen's team were able to draw lessons from what was already hailed as one of the best Scottish courses.

As another pay-and-play resort it was important to make it playable for the average club golfer but give options for the better golfer to score well. There are some memorable links holes, such as the short, 304-yard, par-4, 3rd hole with a sloping infinity green that looks quite ready to throw any overhit approach shot into the estuary beyond. Big hitters might fancy driving the green, but then they also face the prospect of playing their next shot from shingle or seaweed.

The chance to stick a ball in the estuary had already come on the preceding hole with a green tucked into a sandy corner at shore's edge on the 550-yard, par-5, 2nd hole. The fairway is wide, but those who want to take on the two-tier green, should take the Rolling Stones' advice and not fade away.

As a complete contrast to the salt spray-blown first three holes, the 4th turns inland and players take aim at Castle Stuart which lies beyond the green of the par-3 hole. They are four of the most inviting opening holes and naturally there is more to come. Castle Stuart Links is divided by the striking art deco-themed clubhouse with the first nine holes to the east and the second nine to the west.

Those who have played both Kingsbarns and Castle Stuart rate the latter above the former, though it is an

Above The par-5, 2nd hole at the renamed Cabot Highlands hugs the shoreline, one of seven holes at the water's edge.

Opposite top The 3rd hole is a very short par-4, but the green demands absolute precision for approach shots to stay on the putting surface.

Opposite bottom The 144-yard, par-3, 11th hole is Cabot Highlands' answer to the Postage Stamp, a short pitch to a small green with danger all around.

incredibly high benchmark. The front nine edges out the back nine for sheer golfing fun at Castle Stuart and the more northerly course appeals because — not being six miles from St Andrews — it doesn't get so busy. For those making the trip to the Highlands, the course could hardly be more convenient for Inverness Airport, which is sited seven miles to the east. And while in the vicinity there is chance to take in Nairn, Royal Dornoch, Golspie, Brora, Tain or even take a trip to Fortrose (1793).

The Cabot group acquired the Castle Stuart course in 2022, rebranding the facility as Cabot Highlands and revealing plans for a second 18-hole course designed

by the ubiquitous Tom Doak. Located on the far side of Castle Stuart, it is named Old Petty after a church on the property and includes an intriguing hole that spans the tidal salt marsh of the Rough Burn. To reinforce the sheer 'highlandness' of this course — apart from the castle there is an old farmhouse, the church and a bothy — there are rumours that Doak has imported a fishing boat to add to the set dressing. So it's no surprise that the logo for the Old Petty course will be the region's distinctive highland cow known affectionately as a 'Hairy Coo'. They have stopped short of giving it a tam o' shanter.

RAILWAY ENTREPRENEURS BUILT
'THE PALACE IN THE SANDHILLS' TO
ATTRACT GOLFERS, BUT THE COURSE
IS THEIR GREAT LEGACY

CRUDEN BAY

CRUDEN BAY, ABERDEENSHIRE, SCOTLAND

South of Peterhead on the rugged Aberdeenshire coast lies the small village of Cruden Bay. There are many things it could be famous for apart from the golf course — above the village there is the ruined Slains Castle, a large sixteenth-century tower house, built by the 9th Earl of Erroll and linked with the Bram Stoker novel *Dracula*. Stoker was a regular visitor between 1893 and 1910 and early chapters of *Dracula* were written in Cruden Bay.

Dr Samuel Johnson and James Boswell were guests at Slains Castle in 1773. Johnson said that, 'no man can see with indifference' the local geological wonder, a deep sea chasm known as Bullers of Buchan. He is unlikely to have played *gowf* on Ward Hill, above the village, but there is evidence it was played around that time in the form of an antique ballot box inscribed Cruden Golf Club 1791.

There is also a winner's medal from a competition played on Ward Hill in 1883 and it is said the ghostly shapes of ancient bunkers, tees and greens can still be made out on the hill above Port Errol. The line of fisherman's cottages that distinguishes Harbour Street in Port Errol look out across the Water of Cruden to the 4th hole on the more recent golf links.

Cruden Bay Golf Club was built as a resort course of its day, possibly inspired by the Rosapenna Hotel in Donegal and a forerunner to Turnberry and Gleneagles. The links were commissioned in 1894 by the Great North of Scotland Railway Company and were to be accompanied by a luxurious hotel. Built of pink granite it was nicknamed 'the Palace in the Sandhills' whereas the Rosapenna had been a timber frame building imported from Scandinavia. They employed the trusted skills of Old Tom Morris (who had also been involved in the creation of Rosapenna, and the mountainous dunes of the County Donegal coast are

Opposite top A burn crosses the long par-5, 13th fairway, to the 13th green (centre, top). To the right are the tees for the 14th hole which skirts the foot of the 'raised beach' 9th hole above.

Opposite bottom Early in the round, there is the challenging par-3, 4th hole overlooking Port Errol and the Water of Cruden. Beyond is Ward Hill and in the distance Slains Castle.

Above The view from the short par-4, 8th hole tee, a chance to open the shoulders before the steep climb to the 9th tee.

echoed at Cruden Bay) to design the course. Apart from the Championship 18 holes, there would be an inner, nine-hole 'ladies course' — from the days when you could say that.

Though the original measured a mere 5,290 yards, by 1908 that had been lengthened to 5,929 yards. The more recent addition of new tees has clocked the distance up to 6,263 yards, not lengthy but there are some distinctly quirky challenges — such as the blind 193-yard, par-3, 15th hole where golfers are given the position of the flag on the green from a diagram on the tee.

It still follows much the same routing as envisaged by Tom Morris, winding its way though a flat figure of eight, with the crossover point just after the 7th hole. By this time players will have negotiated the challenging par-5, 6th hole, driving through a broad cleft in the dunes onto a moonscape of humps and hollows before laying up to approach a green tucked away in a corner, behind a hillock and guarded by a small burn. Watching professionals take the green on in two would be the happiest of ways to spend an afternoon.

Like many of Ireland's links courses, though adjacent, a number of the holes are secluded from their neighbours by towering sandhills giving both respite from the wind and a feeling of intimacy. There are stunning sea views too, none more so than the tee for the 9th hole which is high on the escarpment (or could it be a raised beach) with the furthest back tee resembling the upper deck of a Japanese city driving range.

Cruden Bay is an experience like no other. The hotel is long gone, demolished in 1952 and replaced by a new clubhouse in 1998. The club offers a warm welcome to visitors who might stray up the coast from the far more expensive Royal Aberdeen, particularly Nicolai Højgaard or Thomas Bjørn. In 1012 King Malcolm II of Scotland defeated a Danish army on the land occupied today by the golf course. Cruden derives from the Gaelic *Croch Dain*, or slaughter of Danes.

DUMBARNIE LINKS HAVE A TIMELESS QUALITY THAT BELIES THE FACT THAT THE COURSE ONLY OPENED IN 2020

DUMBARNIE LINKS

UPPER LARGO, FIFE, SCOTLAND

While the majority of famous golf courses bordering the Firth of Forth face north from East Lothian, the links course at Dumbarnie, 12 miles south of St Andrews, faces south. It's a new pay-and-play course, designed by former Ryder Cup player Clive Clark and opened in the spring of 2020. Considering the amount of golf on offer in this corner of Fife it was a bold move to create a new links course so close to Kingsbarns, Lundin Links, Elie, Leven and Crail, and then charge a green fee in excess of a round on the Old Course of St Andrews.

But as almost everyone who has played the course attests, Dumbarnie Links looks and plays like it has always been there. And for those who don't like the stifling etiquette imposed on visitors to some elite courses it is a welcome breath of fresh air.

The links occupies a 350-acre portion of the 5,000-acre Balcarres Estate, with an out-and-back routing which brings holes tantalizingly close to the beach, but not quite making it. The only flirtation with water at Dumbarnie is a typical winding burn that golfers first meet on the opening hole, after a drive down a wide-cut fairway flanked by sand hills.

Two dogleg holes, the 5th and 15th, offer a split fairway from the tee — the shorter route requires a greater carry from the tee shot, but offers a more direct route to the flag.

Above **Members of Team USA on the 3rd green at Dumbarnie prior to the Walker Cup at St Andrews in 2023.**

Right **Veteran photographer David Cannon enjoys his visits to Dumbarnie Links as it has a nature reserve next door and is home to the Common.**

Opposite top **An aerial view of the 157-yard, par-3, 8th hole, with the 464-yard, par 4, 9th hole beyond.**

Opposite bottom **Stacy Lewis of the United States plays her tee shot on the 1st during the opening round of the Trust Golf Women's Scottish Open at Dumbarnie Links in August 2021.**

There are quite a few contoured greens, including what many describe as its signature hole, the 462-yard, 17th which plays uphill to a heavily bunkered three-tier green that lies beyond a 300-year-old stone wall. Shades of 'Pit' at North Berwick.

It is a course with many wide fairways, built to enjoy rather than test, playing between 5,300 and 6,900 yards depending on the colour of the tee. It has been carved out to emulate courses that were fashioned by nature rather than digger — but given a little bit more room. Already it has attracted the Women's Scottish Open and in 2023 served as a practice course for the American Walker Cup team prior to their match on the Old Course, which the United States won by three points. Given that the Alfred Dunhill Links Championship plays across Kingsbarns, St Andrews and Carnoustie, and that Carnoustie is vulnerable to flooding (and can torture amateurs in what is a pro-am event) it would be no surprise to see Dumbarnie pop up in the trio instead.

Opposite top An aerial view of the opening holes at Durness with the 1st/10th green directly below camera.

Opposite bottom Durness's answer to Turnberry's 'Bruce's Castle' hole. A par-3 tee shot across a rocky bay, with the clubhouse to the right.

Above The 9th/18th green with Balnakiel Beach beyond.

DURNESS GOLF CLUB

BALNAKEIL, DURNESS, SUTHERLAND, SCOTLAND

Durness is not all about the golf. It's also the journey. Situated close to Cape Wrath on the North Western tip of Scotland, it's a whole 260 miles from Edinburgh. The route north to Durness takes in a scenic driving experience to be found in every 'Remarkable Road Trip' guide alongside such classics as Route 66, the Stelvio Pass and the Wild Atlantic Way. Take the North Coast 500 from Lairg and you will drive through stunning moorland, mountain and coastal scenery until you stumble upon Durness. Eventually.

Then there's the golf to play. Durness is a nine-hole course, with another nine tees to create an 18-hole round. It was the inspiration of three local golf enthusiasts Lachie Ross, Ian Morrison and Francis Keith, who opened their 'If you build it, they will come' dream course in 1988.

The first two and last two holes overlook the unspoiled sands of Balnakeil Beach and the isolated ruin of Balnakeil church and its cemetery, with the remaining holes laid out further inland on rugged hilltop terrain around Loch Lanlish.

This is one of the many Western Isles courses with a small, irregularly manned clubhouse, and so golfers must arrive with cash for the honesty box. Instructions as follows: 'Lift the Lid. Inside you will find green fee tickets, plastic envelopes and scorecards (with map on back). Fill in a ticket, put it in an envelope with appropriate fee and post through the Letterbox (That is the slot above box!) Many Thanks. Enjoy your golf.'

The course is 2,753 yards from its longest tees and features six modest par-4s, a single par-5 that sweeps around Loch Lanlish to the green and two par-3s. Like the courses of Old Tom Morris's day, the fairways are moulded to the topography of the land, with the tees and greens the only obvious imposition on this natural landscape.

Without question, the best is saved for last at Durness. Emerging from holes up country, the 8th hole is played downhill to a green perched on the cliff edge. The final par-3 9th hole is played across a craggy, wave-lashed inlet. It's a shorter, less scary version of 'Bruce's Castle' at Turnberry. There may be no lighthouse beyond, only the rolling dunes of Faraid Head (that are just begging to be made into a second nine), but £25 for a round is considerably less than the £425 golfers would have to pay for the Ailsa Course. Pick your day, though. It's not called Cape Wrath for nothing.

FLUNG OUT INTO THE WATERS OF THE
MORAY FIRTH, GOLFERS NOT ONLY
HAVE SEA VIEWS, THEY CAN ALSO
SPOT DOLPHINS

FORTROSE AND ROSEMARKIE
FORTROSE, ROSS AND CROMARTY, SCOTLAND

The older Scottish golf clubs are never shy about proclaiming their heritage and if you ever found yourself wondering what the 15th oldest golf club in the world looked like, then the search stops here, it's Fortrose and Rosemarkie (1793). Located on the north side of the Moray Firth, facing across the water to Castle Stuart (now Cabot Highlands), it occupies a narrow, exposed peninsula named Chanonry Point.

With little transport available in the Victorian era, it was a course for locals and the odd military man rowing across the Moray Firth from the imposing Fort George on the opposite shore. There was no clubhouse till 1895 and so

members would leave their clubs in the care of the governor
of the Black Isle Poor House nearby.

The First World War led to a reduction in members and
also great irritation that the Highland Cyclist Battalion, who
used the clubhouse as a guardhouse, left it in a complete
shambles. By 1924 the club was thriving again and members
could extend the course to 18 holes. In 1932 they invited
the great James Braid to advise on a new layout. With the
addition of more land to lengthen holes, the James Braid
routing is very much still in play.

The road to Chanonry Point divides the course neatly in
two, with the first four holes hugging the coastline on the
Inverness side of the peninsula, as players make their way

out to the lighthouse. The 5th hole, 'Icehouse,' is a short,
133-yard, par-3 that links the two sides of the spit, and
then the 6th, 7th and 8th hug the seaward shore as players
head back inland. Then they double back to the lighthouse,
and when they get there, double back to the clubhouse. If
members are lucky, they can look out to sea and spot the
pod of dolphins that frequent the waters around the point.
The final hole is a testing, long par-3 known as 'Fiery Hillock',
the tee of which is emblazoned with that familiar 1793 date.

Sadly there is no hole named for Miss Isa Ross, who lent
the club money to build a new clubhouse in 1959 and to the
committee's astonishment waived the loan.

GLENEAGLES HAS REMAINED TRUE TO ITS FOUNDER'S VISION WITH THREE OF THE WORLD'S BEST GOLF COURSES AND A PRESTIGIOUS HOTEL

GLENEAGLES
AUCHTERADER, PERTH, SCOTLAND

Donald Matheson's vision of Gleneagles was a long time in the realization. As Engineer-in-Chief of the Caledonian Railway Company, he would have been aware of the Turnberry Hotel's 1906 success in developing a spectacular golf course, attached to a large hotel, close to a railway line. While holidaying in the highlands near Strathearn in 1908, he was reminded of the beauty of his native Perthshire. The land around Gleneagles was the perfect mountain setting for a game of golf; it would surely make a fabulous moorland track with sweeping views of the Ochil Hills and the peaks of Ben Vorlich and the Trossachs... and Gleneagles was very close to the Caledonian Railway's Stirling to Perth line.

He was appointed General Manager of the Caledonian in 1910 and set about his plan for 'a palace in the glens', building a luxury country house hotel complete with a choice of golf courses to attract wealthy first-class clientele. Plans were put on hold during World War I, but despite war-time restrictions on labour, the smaller Queen's Course was completed in 1917 and in 1919 former Open champion James Braid was able to put the finishing touches to the King's Course.

It was not until the hotel's opening in June 1924, with a gala ball featuring band leader Henry Hall and broadcast by BBC Radio, that Gleneagles took its place in the social scene of the 'Roaring Twenties'. The hotel was a success, and the golf course, particularly the King's Course, received generous plaudits.

It had already hosted a major golf event. In 1920 *Golf Illustrated* magazine had promoted the idea of sponsoring a team of 12 to 20 American professional golfers to take part in the Open Championship. It rankled circulation manager James D. Harnett that many British players had won the US Open, but no Americans had won the Open, largely because of the considerable expense of travelling to Britain and the

less-than-generous prize money on offer from tournament organizers the R&A.

In 1921, a team of 12 was due to play in a warm-up tournament at Gleneagles which was announced as the *Glasgow Herald* 1000 Guinea Tournament. It would be the precursor to the Ryder Cup. The American professionals would go on to play the Open at St. Andrews, two weeks later. Ultimately the teams were reduced to ten a side, with five foursomes in the morning and ten singles in the afternoon. Great Britain won by nine matches to three, with three matches halved. Harnett got his wish. The Open that year was won by Jock Hutchinson, born in St Andrews, but who had become a naturalized US citizen in 1920.

With the outbreak of World War II the hotel closed and in time became a military hospital and subsequently a rehabilitation centre for miners. It was open for business again in 1947 and has never looked back, hosting both golfers, grouse shooters and, in 2008, a G8 Summit. It is one of the few golf resorts with a two-star Michelin Restaurant, the Andrew Fairlie, one of only two in Scotland.

More importantly the golf has been supplemented by an extra course. The Jack Nicklaus-designed PGA Centenary Course opened in 1993. Nicklaus called it, "the finest parcel of land in the world I have ever been given to work with."

Almost 20 years later he was back to tinker with his design ahead of the 2014 Ryder Cup. Jack remarked: "With the equipment and the golf ball and everything going so much further it needed alterations. The 18th hole was the biggest change. We dropped the green five or six metres and created a tremendous amphitheatre. It's more about creating good golf than creating the most difficult shots and course in the world. It's about creating one that the guys will enjoy — and I think they will enjoy it." At least the victorious Europeans did.

There were significant tweaks to the Queen's Course in 2017 to return it (a neat 100 years later) to the course that James Braid had intended. Over time, the rough had encroached on fairway width to the extent that fairway bunkers found themselves sitting in the rough. They have now been considerably widened, along with the rebuilding of 89 bunkers. There has also been a drive to add more native heather to the course, reflecting the Caledonian landscape of gorse, Scots pine, silver birch and rowan.

With three fine courses all rated within the world's top 100 it's hard to disagree with Lee Trevino. Standing on the first tee of the King's Course he remarked: "If heaven is as good as this, I sure hope they have some tee times left".

HEBRIDEAN GOLF IS AS MUCH ABOUT THE JOURNEY AS THE GAME AND THE ISLE OF HARRIS COURSE IS A PRIME DESTINATION

ISLE OF HARRIS GOLF CLUB

SCARISTA, LEWIS AND HARRIS, SCOTLAND

You are unlikely to find a Porsche Taycan with a local number plate in the small car park of the Isle of Harris Golf Club. This is golf as it was meant to be, an unostentatious battle with the elements and topography in a remote and rugged part of Scotland that could easily have been the setting for Bill Forsyth's 1983 film *Local Hero*.

The nine-hole Isle of Harris Golf Club is to be found at Scarista, one of five courses in the Outer Hebrides each with its own particular charm. At Barra the greens are protected from gazing sheep with access to the greens by gate. The greens of Benbecula make Troon's Postage Stamp look over-generous and then there is Askernish on South Uist. Askernish was created by Old Tom Morris in 1891 and then neglected as the population of the Western Isles dwindled. It was revived after heroic restoration work and re-opened in 2008 as a playable museum piece, true to the spirit of the game and traditional course maintenance.

The Isle of Harris course dates to 1912 when Alick Marling of Aberdeen, made the journey to the largest Hebridean island to lay out a nine-hole golf course. The club itself was not formed until 1930, but war intervened and play halted, course closed. Presaging what would happen further south, it was reopened by a hardy band of enthusiasts in 1985, allowing visitors once more to play off the incredible surface of machair, or springy turf.

Today, the course measures a none-too-taxing 2,454 yards from the furthest tees, playing to a par of 34. The joy of an uncongested course allows visitors time to take in the views. If the sun is shining, the waters of the bay can be turquoise, as though it were transplanted to a tropical paradise.

SOME DOUBTED THE WISDOM OF CREATING AN EXPENSIVE NEW COURSE SO CLOSE TO ST ANDREWS WITH ITS ABUNDANCE OF GOLFING ACREAGE...

KINGSBARNS GOLF LINKS

KINGSBARNS, FIFE, SCOTLAND

Kingsbarns was the first new Scottish course of the twenty-first century — and it was a good start. Opened in July 2000, only six miles down the coast from St Andrews, golf had been played on and off at Kingsbarns for two centuries. Play had been noted on the site from 1793, a fact reinforced by the formation of the Kingsbarns Golfing Society in 1815. Members played on a nine-hole course, which closed for an undisclosed reason in 1850.

Willie Auchterlonie, honorary professional to the R&A for nearly a quarter of a century, laid out the course again in 1922, but play was interrupted by World War II, when the foreshore was viewed as a possible invasion site and the golf course mined. It then lay fallow as common pasture until coming under the shrewd gaze of American golf course developer Mark Parsinen in the mid-1990s.

Parsinen knew that for an expensive seaside golf course to be successful, golfers wanted more than an expanse of water to gaze out on, they wanted a varied coastline to play around. St Andrews and Muirfield may have been storied courses, but there was just a glimpse of the sea. With almost two miles of shoreline, Kingsbarns hugs the coast like it does at Turnberry.

Architect Kyle Phillips did his homework on a variety of Scottish courses including Royal Dornoch, to make sure

Above An aerial view encompassing most of the Kingsbarns course, with the 2nd green at bottom right. Players then tackle the 515-yard, par-5, 3rd hole taking them along the shoreline to the edge of the property before doubling back.

Opposite top Looking back at the green on the par-4, 7th hole at Kingsbarns.

Opposite bottom The tee shot facing players on what many consider to be Kingsbarns' 'signature' hole, the par-3 15th.

the outcome would look authentic. To fit with Parsinen's brief there are many raised tees giving great sea views and round-halting photo opportunities. The fairways have all the humps and hollows and ripples of a vintage links. In the course of the earth moving, diggers uncovered a new burn, the Cambo, which was welcomed into the layout by the designers, less so by the golfers.

Master golf architect Tom Doak thought it was the best new course in Scotland for 50 years. 'As a piece of construction work, Kingsbarns is one of the best projects I've ever seen,' he wrote in *The Confidential Guide to Golf Courses* (2014). 'It started out as a flat field above a small bowl of links land, but I wouldn't have believed that

if I hadn't seen it for myself, because the reshaping and grassing of the landscape was so well done.'

Favourite holes for many are the par-5, 12th and the par-3, 15th, which are both perilously close to the sea's edge. The 12th curves round to a green at the eastern end of the property, while the 15th has a tee below a stand of pines and the shot needs to carry over a small inlet. It may not be as dramatic as Turnberry or as good value as Durness, but it is still a hole to set the pulse racing.

A round at Kingsbarns may not be the quickest, but it is certainly the chance to measure up against one of the modern greats at a club where the customer, not the long-time member is king.

OLD TOM MORRIS HAD A LARGE HAND IN CREATING A FRONT NINE THAT MATCHES THE VERY BEST SCOTLAND HAS TO OFFER

MACHRIHANISH

MACHRIHANISH, ARGYLL, SCOTLAND

Like Durness and the Isle of Harris, the links course at Machrihanish is one of those where the journey to the course is part of the experience. Travellers wishing to explore the unspoiled peninsular that inspired Paul McCartney — who spent summers at High Park Farm near Campbeltown — will find the Scotland of 30 years ago.

The links started life In 1876 as the Kintyre Golf Club playing over ten holes, was extended to 12 and then Old Tom Morris was invited to take the steamer from Ardrossan to Campbeltown in 1879 and run his eye over the place. It's been reported that Old Tom declared: 'The Almichty Maun had gowf in his e'e when he made this place.'

He added a further six holes to the traditional out-and-back links that curves around Machrihanish Beach, but most importantly added the first, 'Battery', a drive across the corner of the beach where players can choose the precise angle of their bravery. In 2009 Jack Nicklaus described it as the best opening hole in golf, 120 years after Old Tom had come up with the idea.

Indeed, the front nine is rated as one of the best Scotland has to offer, played through a rolling hummocky dunescape quite unlike the flatland of the first hole. While some links courses are routed between dunes, Old Tom and his predecessors were not ones for footling around and have clambered over them. Many of the fairways resemble interlocking spurs of rumpled green velvet. Drive down the centre of the fairway on the par-4, 7th hole, 'Bruach More' and you are unlikely to find your ball in the centre of the short stuff. This is true of most links courses, but seems particularly true of Machrihanish.

For the integrity of the golf played here, a round of the Championship Course is tremendous value for money and for those whose appetites have been whetted, there is also the prospect of a round at Machrihanish Dunes next door.

Opposite **Two views over the 5th and 11th greens at sunset, with the 5th green to the right and the 6th tee in the foreground.**

Above **The green on the par-4, 18th hole with the clubhouse of The Honourable Company of Edinburgh Golfers beyond. That rake needs moving.**

MUIRFIELD

GULLANE, EAST LOTHIAN, SCOTLAND

Muirfield may not be the most spectacular golf course to look at, but Jack Nicklaus is of the firm belief that it is the best in Britain. His view may be coloured by the fact he won his first Open Championship here in 1966, but the Golden Bear cites more compelling reasons: 'It requires a player to play almost every club in the bag, and it tests every part of the game.'

Jack also believes it is the *fairest* test of golf played on the Open rota, for very good reason. When Old Tom Morris created the original course in 1891 he was constrained by the modest walled-in acreage leased by the Honourable Company of Edinburgh Golfers. They had lost patience with Leith Links, had found Musselburgh increasingly busy, so voted to build their own course on leased land.

By 1922 they had bought the property outside Gullane and another 50 acres, which allowed a striking new approach to Old Tom's original course. Instead of going out and back in the St Andrews Old Course manner, Harry Colt produced a layout where the opening nine holes progress around the perimeter of the property in a clockwise circle,

and then the closing nine holes run anti-clockwise on an inner circuit. Thus when the wind blows — a very likely occurrence on the East Lothian coast — players will have to adapt to it arriving from every direction.

The pedigree of winners of Open Championships hosted at Muirfield is testament to the challenge it presents: Vardon, Hagen, Perry, Cotton, Player, Nicklaus, Trevino, Watson, Faldo, Els and Phil Mickelson are all multiple major winners who have mastered Gullane's most famous course.

There are two par-5 holes and two par-3s in each circle of nine (of which the 13th is deemed the trickiest test) and only one blind drive, on the 11th hole. Even then the fairway landing areas are reasonably flat; so unlike many links courses, the ball will end up more or less where you expected. It may not have golfers constantly reaching for the camera every hole, the inspiration comes from the variety and ingenuity of challenges thrown in a player's path — some might say a coastal version of Pine Valley. It's not for nothing that Jack exported it to Ohio.

Opposite top Looking down on Musselburgh's venerable course. The first tee is bottom left, outside the rails and players drive across the course to the par-3 green, bottom right.

Opposite bottom A view from the far end of the course with the 4th green at the base of the photo, with its fairway running parallel to the rails.

MUSSELBURGH LINKS, THE OLD COURSE

MUSSELBURGH, EAST LOTHIAN, SCOTLAND

Hardly a *lang whack* outside Edinburgh, the Old Course at Musselburgh was once declared the oldest of them all. Golf courses within race courses are like flat-roofed pubs — modern, soulless and to be avoided if possible. But only one has the status of being a former Open Championship venue, and that is the great Musselburgh Links. Not to be confused with the Royal Musselburgh Golf Club, a fine inland course with a baronial hall of a clubhouse, Musselburgh distinguishes itself by adding 'The Old Course' to its title.

Until 2016, Musselburgh Links was the officially certified, *Guinness Book of World Records* Oldest Golf Course in the World. Written evidence came from the records of Sir John Foulis of Ravelston, a prominent Edinburgh lawyer, who played golf at Musselburgh in 1672. He wagered a substantial sum of money in a match with his friends Gosford and Lyon across the links and recorded the details. 'March 2 Lost at Golfe at Musselboorgh with Gosford, Lyon etc ... £3 5s 0d,' (a hefty £600 today).

Golf was recorded as being played at St Andrews far earlier, but there was no written evidence as to exactly where around the town it took place. When a legal document was finally unearthed in 2016, the R&A heaved a sigh of relief that the official title could revert to the Old Course.

Musselburgh had started life as a seven-hole course before being surrounded by the racing rails in 1816. The land was common land and the council decided to back both the popular sporting pastimes. An eighth hole was added in 1832 and a ninth, the Sea Hole, added in 1870, but further expansion would prove impossible.

Nevertheless, the introduction of horse racing didn't stop the course from hosting the Open Championship six times between 1874 and 1889. Played over four rounds of nine holes, the first was won by Scotland's Mungo Park who collected £8, the last by Willie Park Junior in an all-Scotland top ten.

A further claim to fame for Musselburgh, which has not been rescinded, is the size of golf holes. In 1829 they employed an automatic hole cutter four and a quarter inches (108mm) in diameter which was subsequently adopted by the R&A as the standard width of a golf cup.

Left An aerial view of the 433-yard par-4, 2nd hole, 'Sea'. The par-4, 3rd hole, 'Trap' stretches beyond, while the 16th hole, 'Gate', on the homeward nine, passes right in front of the Marine Hotel at North Berwick.

ONE OF THE GAME'S OLDEST COURSES HAS GIVEN GOLF A CLASSIC PAR-3 HOLE COPIED BY GOLF ARCHITECTS THE WORLD OVER

NORTH BERWICK WEST LINKS

NORTH BERWICK, EAST LOTHIAN, SCOTLAND

North Berwick is one of Scotland's classic East Coast courses, looking out across the Firth of Forth to the great mass of Bass Rock and Europe's biggest colony of gannets. Patronized by the gentlemen golfers of East Lothian, like many of the old Scottish courses, golf was played on the land that constitutes North Berwick's West Links long before it was officially acknowledged.

There is reference to golf being played here as early as 1605, but it was not until 1832 that the North Berwick Golf Club formalized arrangements to play on the six-hole course, extending to the March Dyke stone wall. By that time, St Andrews had reduced their 22-hole course to 18 and so medal competitions on the West Links could include three circuits of the six holes.

Over time the East Lothian course was extended beyond the common land, to seven, then nine and then 18 holes as the game's respectability and popularity increased. A constant criticism of the course was that it was too short. It was in 1868 that land was developed for what would

Above Looking along the line of the protective stone wall in front of the 13th hole, 'Pit'.

Right David Cannon's long lens finds a hare lingering in the safety of the long grass at North Berwick.

Opposite top An aerial view of the green on the 190-yard, par-3, 15th hole, 'Redan'. The line into the green is by the corner of the bunker at left.

become the West Links' most copied hole by generations of golf course architects.

'Redan' is an 190-yard, par-3 hole with an elevated, contoured green angled at 45 degrees to the tee with a large bunker guarding the front shoulder of the green. It was named by a British army officer returning from the Crimean War, who likened the angle of the green to a military redan, a defensive position similarly angled against the point of attack. The great Alister MacKenzie used Redan in his design for the 6th hole at Augusta National, and you can find tuition on the best way to play a 'redan'.

Other celebrated holes include 'Perfection', so-named because members thought it would take two perfect shots

to get on the green (presumably without a North Sea gale blowing) and 'Pit', which is a short par-4 which requires an approach shot that hops over a stone wall to a very small green. The BBC's Ken Brown, famous for 'Ken on the Course' describes it thus: "Look at the green, it's so skinny. And the wall, it frightens you. It's magical, it's golden, it's fantastic. Quirky and unique, golfing genius."

Although the original part of the course was played across common sheep and cattle pasturage, thus under the jurisdiction of the local council, the rest of the course was still leased. In 1953, the proprietor of the Westerdunes Hotel offered to buy out the privately owned holes and extend the course further west into the Archerfield Estate. There had

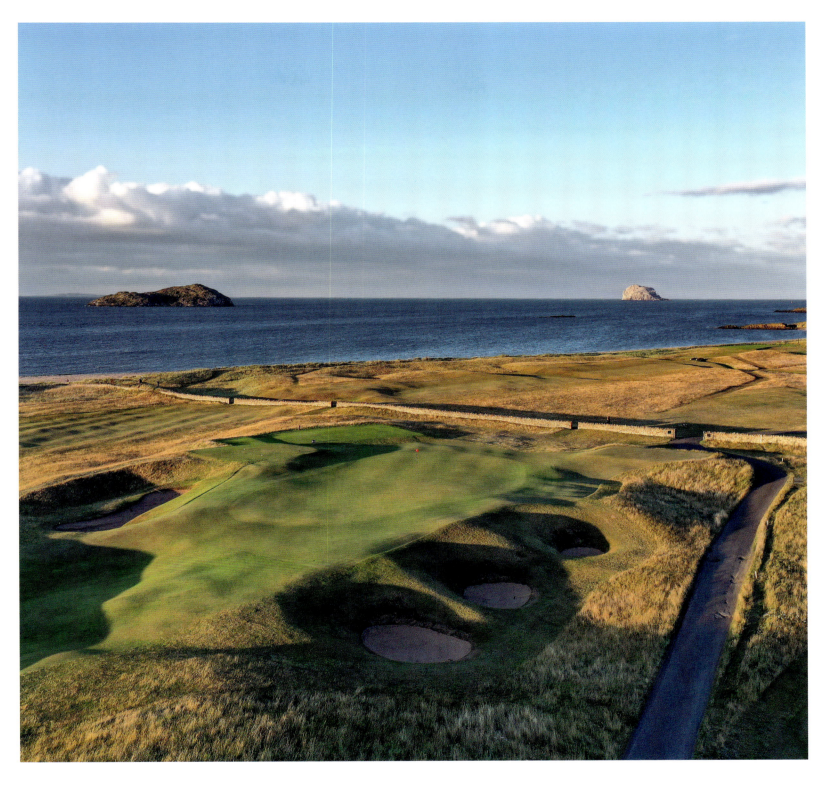

been the 13-hole Fidra Golf Course there since 1869.

Fidra had been enlarged to 18 holes by North Berwick's golf professional Ben Sayers around 1910, but much of the course had fallen into disrepair after being commandeered by the army in World War II. Thus on one stretch of Scottish coastline there was Muirfield to the west, North Berwick to the east and jammed between them the Fidra course. North Berwick's town council intervened to protect their local golf clubs and bought the land in 1954 to safeguard their sporting heritage.

Like St Andrews, a number of clubs have access to the municipal links, The North Berwick Golf Club (founded 1832), Tantallon Golf Club (founded 1853), Bass Rock Golf Club (founded 1873) and The North Berwick Ladies' Golf Club (founded 1888), though management of the course is by the oldest member.

Although they are neighbours, Muirfield and the North Berwick have their own distinctive character. The West Links is much shorter at 6,420 yards but still a par 71 and is a proper seaside links course, while Muirfield turns inland and is much longer. Together with Gullane, (just west of Muirfield) and the restored Fidra/Archerfield Links they form a quartet of golf courses to rival those along 17-mile drive in Monterrey. For many, though, the West Links is the most enjoyable to play, with lenient rough, two of the most famous holes in golf and views that inspire.

THE CHAMPIONSHIP COURSE WAS SHAPED BY DONALD ROSS, A SON OF DORNOCH, WHO WENT ON TO SHAPE MANY AMERICAN COURSES

ROYAL DORNOCH

DORNOCH, SUTHERLAND, SCOTLAND

Scotland's elite modern courses — Kingsbarns, Cabot Highlands and Dumbarnie are the direct descendants of Royal Dornoch. It is this ancient course in Sutherland, 43 miles north of Inverness on the edge of the Dornoch Firth that provided the template for many of the elements that go to make the perfect round of links golf. All of the above named courses strive to look as though they have been around forever. Which Royal Dornoch has.

Evidence of its ancient past came from the 1616 financial records of Sir Robert Gordon — for historical context, this was just five years after Shakespeare had written *A Winter's Tale*. Tasked with the tutelage of his nephew John Gordon, the 13th Earl of Sutherland, Sir Robert detailed the equipment bought for his young charge: 'Item ten poundis guven this year for bowes, arrows, golf clubbes and balles'. He later observed of Royal Dornoch: 'About this toun, along the sea road there are the fairest and lairgest links of any pairt of Scotland'.

Four hundred years later, that is still true. Like so many historic clubs of the British Isles, Dornoch benefitted from the touch of the Grand Old Man of Golf, Tom Morris.

In 1886 he surveyed the nine-hole course and added another nine holes to make the full 18. Once complete he played an almost perfect round at 65 years of age and declared of the links: 'There canna be better for gowf'.

Other golf luminaries have contributed to this hallowed ground, including J.H. Taylor and Donald Ross, extending the course well beyond Old Tom's 5,285 yards and adding another 18 holes, the Struie Course, on the 'Common Good land of the Royal Burgh'.

The Championship Course is breathtakingly beautiful but not an easy one. Many of the greens are elevated and quite a few domed, so missing them and getting up and down in two is not easy. This particular facet is attributed to Dornoch's most famous son, Donald Ross. Ross held the position of head greenkeeper and professional and after emigrating to the United States embarked on a career of golf course design. Those professionals struggling at Pinehurst No.2 in the 2024 US Open might have been advised to play Royal Dornoch first. Many of Ross's designs, of which Pinehurst is one, bear the hallmark of Royal Dornoch's greens.

FAMED FOR ITS POSTAGE STAMP PAR-3, TROON IS ONE OF THE MANY COURSES ORIGINALLY LAID OUT BY OLD TOM MORRIS

Above **The shortest hole on the Open rota, the par-3 'Postage Stamp' where Chile's Joaquin Niemann came unstuck at the 2024 Open. He carded a quintuple-bogey 8 after finding three different bunkers.**

ROYAL TROON

TROON, AYRSHIRE, SCOTLAND

Troon was a late starter in the Open Championship rota compared to its next-door neighbour Prestwick. Golf had been played over the links at Prestwick for many years before the club was founded in 1851. The original course there was laid out by Old Tom Morris who put together a challenging 12 holes amounting to 3,799 yards. When the

acknowledged 'Greatest Golfer' Allan Robertson died in 1859, Prestwick organized the Open Championship to find out his successor — the three rounds of twelve holes were completed in a single day. Eight golfers contested the event, with Willie Park Senior winning the championship by two shots from Old Tom Morris. Prestwick would go on to host

56

the Open Championship for the next 10 years and 24 times in total.

Royal Troon's Old Course started modestly with just five holes in 1878, but by 1888 professionals George Strath and Willie Fernie had enlarged it to 18. It was far longer than Prestwick and more of a challenge, designed in the traditional out-and-back manner of the Old Course at St Andrews. When it managed to elbow its way onto the Open rota in 1923 the club asked five-time Champion Golfer James Braid to redesign a number of the holes.

The front nine holes are a gentle prelude, a series of short par-4s coasting along the foreshore, before the back nine take their toll. They include the 601-yard, par-5, 6th,

'Turnberry' (Turnberry haven't returned the favour and named one of their holes 'Troon') which was the longest in Open history until Royal Liverpool at Hoylake trumped them in 2023.

Then there is the hole everyone remembers, the 123-yard, 8th hole, Postage Stamp, the shortest in Open history, with unsurprisingly one of the smallest greens. Its given name was 'Ailsa' but after retired professional Willie Park Jr. referred to the hole in *Golf Illustrated* as: 'A pitching surface skimmed down to the size of a postage stamp,' the name stuck. Twenty-one-year-old American professional Gene Sarazen made his Open debut at Troon in 1923. He returned to play in the tournament many times, but in 1973, at the

age of 71, and playing with fellow veteran Max Faulkner, he scored a hole in one. The following day, the man who had invented the sand wedge holed his bunker shot for a two at the same hole.

After the turn there is the 'Railway' hole, the 11th, a long par-4 hole with Out of Bounds along the railway line which runs parallel to the fairway on the right. The 17th, 'Rabbit', is the most difficult of the short holes at 218 yards and can require a driver if the wind is strong and head on. The plateau green falls away sharply on both sides and is well guarded by bunkers.

Despite the success of the 1923 competition at Troon, when the Open returned to neighbours Prestwick in 1925 there was chaos. The sheer numbers in the crowd overwhelmed the marshals with spectators encroaching on the rough and players' shots regularly getting deflected either favourably or unfavourably. Leading golf writer Bernard Darwin reported that the course's cramped layout made it difficult to host large galleries and doubted that the tournament would ever be held at Prestwick again. He was right. Troon which had enough space to establish a 'New' course, the Portland, in 1895 (redesigned by Alister MacKenzie in 1921) disappeared off the Open rota as well.

However in 2024 it celebrated its 10th hosting of the event with a fine win for Xander Schauffele, who shot a final-round 65 to win his second major championship, two strokes ahead of Justin Rose and 54-hole leader Billy Horschel.

It wasn't quite the James Braid Old Course they played on. Ahead of the 2016 Open, won by Henrik Stenson after an epic duel with Phil Mickelson, leading golf architects Mackenzie & Ebert had made minor adjustments to almost every hole, especially the 9th, 10th and 15th. The backdrop of a line of low, wind-blown trees behind the 9th green bordering the caravan park had been replaced by a long grassy berm and with a massive bunker installed to the left of the green.

Although Royal Troon is a private club, it is possible for guests to play either the Old Course or the Portland, which has its own separate clubhouse. In addition there is the Craigend Course, a nine-hole, par-3 challenge. 'Craigend' is also the name of the testing final hole on the Old Course, which along with the Portland was built across the Craigend Farm grazing land. In all there are 45 holes to tackle, a whole 40 more than were first contemplated back in 1878.

IT IS A CREDIT TO ST ANDREWS THAT THE WORLD'S MOST FAMOUS GOLF COURSE CAN BE PLAYED FOR A REASONABLE GREEN FEE

ST ANDREWS OLD COURSE

ST ANDREWS, FIFE, SCOTLAND

St Andrews is awash with golf courses. To the north of the city there's the Eden Course, the Balgove Course, the New Course, the Jubilee Course, the Strathtyrum Course, and of course, that venerable institution, the Old Course.

Until recently the self-proclaimed Home of Golf had a dilemma. It was well known that golf had been played in this corner of Fife since the sixteenth century, but there was no documentary evidence as to where that ancient golf was played. Thus the *Guinness Book of World Records* attributed the Oldest Golf Course accolade to Musselburgh to the east of Edinburgh.

Mercifully, in 2016 a researcher uncovered a charter from 1552 issued by the Archbishop of St Andrews, John Hamilton, granting that the links land could be used for grazing animals, drying clothes and golf. There was a collective sigh of relief across the Firth of Forth. The pastime had already been documented for a century, as Scotland under King James II had issued a ban in 1457 preventing men from playing the game when they should have been practising martial skills, such as archery. The ban remained in force for 50 years but was rescinded by James IV who enjoyed the game himself.

That common ownership established in 1552 remains to this day. The 'Old Lady' is a public course over common land. The Royal and Ancient Golf Club of St Andrews may have a grand clubhouse by the first tee, but it is just one of many clubs that continue to have playing privileges on the course. Elsewhere in the city one can find clubhouses of St Regulus Ladies Golf Club, St Andrews Golf Club, The New Golf Club, and The St Rule Club.

The 'golfing ground' on the links only became referred to as the Old Course after 1895 when the New Course was built. Before that it was very much a case of a course evolution over time. In 1764 there were 22 holes and the

members would play to the same green going out, as they would coming in. It was the Captain of the Gentlemen Golfers who made a seismic change to the structure of golf that year. William St Clair of Roslin thought that the first four and last four holes on the course were too short. His plan to cut that number in half was approved by the committee and St Andrews became 18 holes, a number both replicated and halved across the golfing spectrum. A century later, local club-maker and the outstanding golfer of his day, Allan Robertson, is said to have created a 17th green separate from the first. This gave the current 18-hole layout seven enormous double greens, some almost an acre in size, and four single greens – the 1st, 9th, 17th and 18th.

History and landmarks abound at St Andrews. The Society of St Andrews Golfers was given royal patronage by King William IV in 1834 and changed their name to the Royal and Ancient Golf Club, who then became custodians of the rules of golf. Their Victorian clubhouse was built in 1853, several hundred years after the Swilcan Bridge was built over the Swilcan Burn crossing the 18th fairway.

The 17th, the 'Road' hole, is one of the most famously antagonistic closing holes in golf, with the Out of Bounds beyond the green, over a road and a wall, which professionals have been known to bounce a short shot against to ricochet onto the putting surface. The Road hole bunker has the gravitational pull of a black hole.

Opposite top A photo taken from the Old Course Hotel looking across to the 2nd and 15th greens.

Opposite bottom The par-5, 14th hole featuring 'Hell Bunker' in the foreground — the forerunner for many troublesome bunkers to be named for Satan. Notably at Pine Valley's 10th.

Above One of the world's most iconic bridges crossing one of the world's most famous final holes. The Swilcan Bridge has helped golfers across the Swilcan burn for centuries past, and will be there for centuries to come.

The 18th hole is generous — a huge, gently rippling fairway up to a monster green, where Constantino Rocca sank a 65-foot putt to tie the 1995 Open with John Daly (but lost the playoff) and Doug Sanders missed a two-foot putt to tie the 1970 Open with Jack Nicklaus (and lost the playoff).

There are notorious bunkers at St Andrews — in 1921 Bobby Jones took four shots to get out of the 'Hill' bunker on the par-3, 11th and promptly tore up his scorecard and left the course. Little could he imagine that St Andrews would go on to make him a freeman of the city and name the 10th hole in his honour. Then there is the 'Hell' bunker protecting the 14th' a larger-than-it-looks trap named for obvious reasons and the 'Deacon Simes' bunker about 30

yards on from the 'Principal's Nose' cluster. It was named for the clergyman after he requested that his ashes be spread in the bunker. He reasoned that he had spent so much time there during his rounds, he might as well spend eternity in it as well. And as for 'Miss Grainger's Bosoms'... well, let's not go there.

The fact that St Andrews, a major championship venue, is open to play through a daily ballot to visiting players from around the world has endeared it to golf's congregation. It may not be the toughest course in the world, but those who have played it say that when their name is announced by the starter on the first tee, it is a spine-tingling moment. Crossing the Swilcan Burn two times and rolling up the Valley of Sin is an essential pilgrimage for every serious golfer.

THE GROWTH OF RAILWAYS ALLOWED DEVELOPERS TO BUILD GRAND HOTELS ATTACHED TO GLORIOUS GOLF COURSES AND ATTRACT THE VERY RICH

TRUMP TURNBERRY

TURNBERRY, AYRSHIRE, SCOTLAND

Scotland's west coast courses do not have the rich historic footprint of the east. Golf in the Victorian era was a gentleman's game and the city of Edinburgh's esteemed professional gentlemen patronized local courses at Musselburgh, Muirfield and North Berwick. The gentlemen of Ayr on the Firth of Clyde to the west had their course at Prestwick (1851), but it was the east coast that had an abundance of heath and dunes and patrons with enough money to afford clubs and losing expensive golf balls.

In the last decade of the nineteenth century, when golf had become the game of the people, the ambition of a landowner/entrepreneur with a vision created the Turnberry Golf Course. Archibald Kennedy, 3rd Marquess of Ailsa, owned extensive properties on the Ayrshire coast, and wanted to develop them. He built a harbour at Maidens to improve the fishing industry, and, as a director of the Glasgow and South Western Railway (G&SWR), rather liked the idea of a branch line from Ayr to Girvan with a private station for his country seat, Culzean Castle.

He also had some unproductive grazing land surrounding the ruin of Robert the Bruce's old castle on the promontory by Turnberry Lighthouse. He came up with the idea of running the branch line, the Maidens and Dunure Light Railway, through Turnberry where he would build a hotel

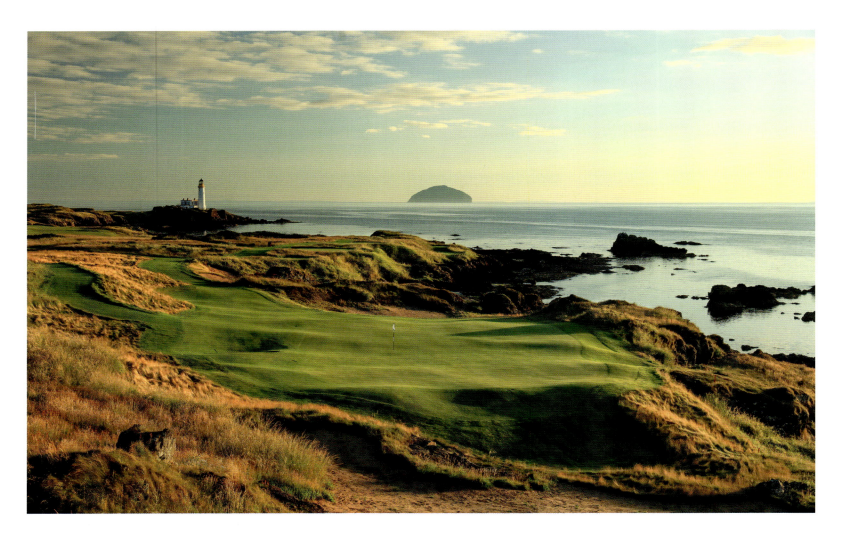

and a golf course on the land that stretched out to the lighthouse.

The elegant, 100-room Turnberry Station Hotel opened on the same day as the branch line, 17 May 1906. The 13-hole golf course, designed by 1883 Open Champion Willie Fernie, the professional at Troon, had been open since 1901 and proven popular. So popular that extra holes were added and a second nine-hole course laid out. The hotel, conveniently close to the railway, was also a hit. But the course's proximity to a rail link made it a perfect location for a military site when war was declared in 1914.

After air strips were built on land to the north of the hotel (and they still exist today, though the King Robert the Bruce course has broken through on its way to the coast) the Royal Flying Corps trained pilots in the art of aerial gunnery and combat, while the Turnberry Hotel was used as a hospital to take wounded men from the Scottish regiments.

It was a pattern repeated in World War II, the Turnberry Hotel closed in October 1939, and the RAF returned in 1941 to rebuild the runways and recommission the site. Once more the hotel became a military hospital.

At war's end the hotel was dilapidated and the course was in a mess. Golf course architect Mackenzie Ross restored the Ailsa course which was reopened in 1951, but with materials shortages, and rationing in the stark, post-war period, the hotel's refurbishment would take a little longer.

Turnberry's greatest coup was to attract the Open Championship for 1977. In the final two days it turned into 'The Duel in the Sun', a head-to-head strokeplay match between the world's greatest golfer, 14-time major winner Jack Nicklaus and the up-and-coming Tom Watson. Paired together for the final two days, they streaked away from the rest of the field beneath a scorching sun. The once-verdant Turnberry course had been rendered yellow, with straw-like rough, yet nobody could get close to Nicklaus and Watson who were slugging it out shot-for-shot.

On the final hole Nicklaus was one behind when he slashed his drive wide into the rough. Watson only had to make par and had one hand on the claret jug when he landed his approach two feet from the flag. But the Golden Bear wasn't finished. He made the green with his recovery shot and sank a huge putt for birdie, sending the crowd wild. But unlike Doug Sanders at St Andrews, Watson didn't miss his short putt to give Jack a reprieve. He had won at −12 to Nicklaus's −11, eight strokes better than any man had ever finished golf's oldest major.

Hubert Green took third place at −1, the only other man to finish under par. Asked for his thoughts on the day's play he smiled: 'I won this golf tournament. I don't know what game those other two guys were playing.'

The Open has been played four times at Turnberry, in 1977, 1986, 1994, and 2009, when Tom Watson almost pulled off another spectacular win at the age of 59,

Opposite On a clear day players can see Ailsa Craig in the south, and to the west, the majestic mountains on the Isle of Arran. A view from behind the par-3 11th green looking back towards the lighthouse and Ailsa Craig.

Above The par-4, 16th hole 'Wee Burn' was renovated as part of the improvements programme on the Ailsa Course.

bogeying the final hole when a par would have made him champion. It's unlikely that the Open will return under the Trump ownership, even though the course has been made significantly better.

Many feared that the Ailsa course would be blanded out when it was bought by the hotelier in 2014, but Trump took advice from the R&A as to who he should hire, and the remodel under golf architect Martin Ebert has been universally acclaimed as a masterpiece, making a great course even better. The revamped course brings the coast more into play between the 6th and 12th holes, which includes the daunting par-3, 9th hole, 'Bruce's Castle' (named after the castle ruin beyond the lighthouse) with a drive from

the back tee of 248 yards across a formidable, craggy bay.

Fittingly, golfers can stop and take their breath at the lighthouse/halfway house before heading off down the 10th, the par-5, 'Dinna Fouter' (Don't mess about) along the coast, before another major flirtation with water on the 11th 'Maidens', which is a mere 215 yards.

The Kintyre course was also remodelled by Martin Ebert and renamed the King Robert the Bruce course, with the nine-hole Arran course making it 45 holes available for golfers with a significant bank balance. A round of the Ailsa course costs in excess of £400/$500, while the sunny conditions that greeted Messrs Nicklaus and Watson can never be guaranteed.

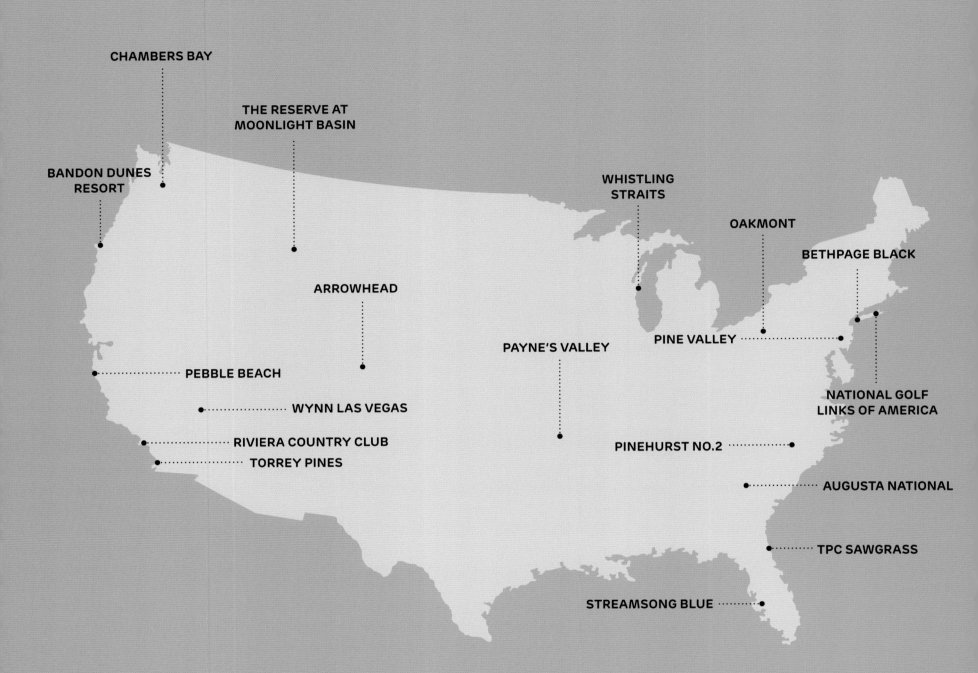

CHAMBERS BAY

THE RESERVE AT
MOONLIGHT BASIN

BANDON DUNES
RESORT

WHISTLING
STRAITS

OAKMONT

BETHPAGE BLACK

ARROWHEAD

PINE VALLEY

PAYNE'S VALLEY

PEBBLE BEACH

NATIONAL GOLF
LINKS OF AMERICA

WYNN LAS VEGAS

RIVIERA COUNTRY CLUB

TORREY PINES

PINEHURST NO.2

AUGUSTA NATIONAL

TPC SAWGRASS

STREAMSONG BLUE

USA

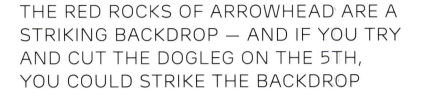

THE RED ROCKS OF ARROWHEAD ARE A STRIKING BACKDROP — AND IF YOU TRY AND CUT THE DOGLEG ON THE 5TH, YOU COULD STRIKE THE BACKDROP

ARROWHEAD

LITTLETON, COLORADO, USA

At last count there were 13 Arrowhead golf courses in the United States, but only one has majestic sandstone formations. Other courses around the world have rocks in play. Lundin Ladies in Fife has Neolithic, carved-granite standing stones dotting the fairways, Leaders Peak in China's Kunming Stone Forest had a course woven between craggy limestone outcrops, but neither are as spectacular as Arrowhead.

Located at Littleton, in sight of Denver, Colorado, the rocks that corral Robert Trent Jones' course (both senior and junior were involved) are part of the Fountain Formation which extends across parts of Colorado, Wyoming, and New Mexico. The famous Red Rocks amphitheatre near Denver is made of the same red-oxide-rich stuff.

At 6,636 yards and a par-70 it's not too rigorous a test, particularly at an elevation of 5,351 ft (1,631 metres) — just over a mile — where golf balls will fly further because of the thin air. At nearby Coors Field baseballs are stored in a humidor to make them heavier and less bouncy and prevent a distortion of home run statistics. Nobody is asking you to store your golf balls in a humidor at Arrowhead.

Some of the notable holes include the 5th which is a short par-4 that doglegs to the right around a large slab of red rock and with the bonus of thinner air is tempting to drive over. All 18 holes are rated for photo ops, but the back nine are esteemed greater than the front nine for golf. The 17th is an 175-yard par-3 where the tee points down a canyon of red rocks to a green with a pond at the rear and a cliff of striking red beyond that. Like dining in a two-star Michelin restaurant when the main course arrives — you've got to take a picture.

73

BOBBY JONES' IDEA TO PROMOTE HIS GEORGIA COURSE HAS BECOME AN UNMISSABLE EVENT ON THE GOLFING CALENDAR

AUGUSTA NATIONAL

AUGUSTA, GEORGIA, USA

Augusta National is one of the hallowed grounds of American sport. Los Angeles has the Coliseum, Boston has Fenway Park, Indianapolis has the Brickyard and Georgia has the course that Bobby Jones established — a relative newcomer from 1933.

Jones, a lawyer by trade, was easily the most successful amateur golfer to play the game. At the height of his powers from 1923 to 1930, he would regularly beat top professionals such as Walter Hagen and Gene Sarazen. That's not to say he was immune from making money from his skill, for the 1926 Open Championship he placed a bet at long odds with British bookmakers that this Yank with the southern drawl would win — which he duly did.

Having retired from the game at 28 he teamed up with financier Clifford Roberts in 1930 to build a world-class course in Georgia that might prove suitable for winter golf. He found a plantation house complete with a 356-acre former plant nursery known as 'Fruitlands' (to put this in perspective, the original Muirfield was 117 acres), enlisted English golf designer Alister MacKenzie and set about creating his perfect course.

MacKenzie, a former army surgeon and World War I expert on camouflage, had helped design more than 70 courses when he arrived in Georgia, having worked on Royal Melbourne and Cypress Point in the preceding years. He was the first significant golf architect who had not been a leading player in his time, but would be helped in his work by 'The Emperor Jones'.

During the first decade of the club's existence, success was not guaranteed. The Masters tournament was proposed as a means of promoting the course, but the PGA, with its historic links to the privileged old-money courses of the

Above Huge crowds gather at the par-3, 16th hole and its imperceptible (from this angle) slope combined with very fast greens can send a ball landing near the pin, to the fringe at right.

Right There is order in everything at Augusta, expressed here in a sea of reserved chairs by the 18th green.

Opposite top Two thirds of Amen Corner on show — the 11th green at left with the tee for the par-3, 12th to its right and the 12th green protected by the magnetic pull of Rae's Creek.

Opposite bottom The tricky putting surface of the 13th green with Augusta's famous azaleas in full bloom.

northeast, was doubtful that Atlanta could provide enough hotel rooms.

Despite all that, the course with its every hole named for a Georgia plant species, charmed the American golf establishment. Bobby Jones came out of retirement to play an exhibition round from the tournament's debut in 1934 until 1948, by which time the Augusta National Invitational had transformed itself into the Masters. MacKenzie never got to see the course in action, dying in January 1934, and like all championship courses his work has been altered and tinkered with many times over the years. The most recent changes in the new millennium were by Tom Fazio who had the essential task of lengthening the yardage to protect the

course's reputation in the era of new tech. This has always been the way in golf. MacKenzie himself redesigned courses to account for the new Haskell wound ball, which bounced and rolled much further than the old gutta-percha golf ball.

Given the care and attention to detail lavished on the course by the groundstaff, the result is one of the most idyllic (to look at) golf courses known to creation. If, as Old Tom Morris references him, 'the Almighty Maun' smiles kindly on Georgia, the profusion of azaleas are in full bloom as the honorary starter — quite often Gary Player — trundles onto the first tee.

In such a manicured environment, familiar to millions of television viewers over the decades, the loss of even a

Above 'Patrons' watch from their official chairs by the 10th green.

Opposite top Max Homa of the United States plays his tee shot on the 18th hole during the final round of the 2024 Masters.

Opposite bottom The trophy awaiting Scottie Scheffler ahead of the 2024 winner's presentation outside the Augusta National clubhouse.

single tree can be a significant event. Dwight D. Eisenhower was an important member of the club from 1948 and during his presidency managed to visit 29 times. He was duly gifted an exclusive cabin on the estate, known obviously as the Eisenhower Cabin. But Ike failed to succeed in an important course alteration. A loblolly pine that came into play from the narrow 17th teeshot was hit by the president so many times that at a 1956 club meeting he asked for it to be cut down. Not wishing to offend the leader of the Western World by saying no, club chairman Clifford Roberts adjourned the meeting. Thence it became known as the 'Eisenhower Tree' and was eventually felled in 2014 after sustaining extensive damage during a rare ice storm.

During the second round of the 2023 tournament, the course lost a further three trees on the 17th. Thankfully, it was late in the day and no spectators were injured as the wind got up and knocked flat three mature Georgia pines.

The greens at Augusta are hard and fast, a firmness assisted by an underground irrigation and ventilation system known as the SubAir System which has been in place since 1994. Apart from the lightning fast putting surface, which players must tiptoe round, there is the infamous Amen Corner to get through. It was a term first used by Herbert Warren Wind in a 1958 *Sports Illustrated* article drawing on a jazz lyric, 'shoutin' in Amen Corner'. Except there is no shouting at Augusta, 'patrons' are kindly requested not to

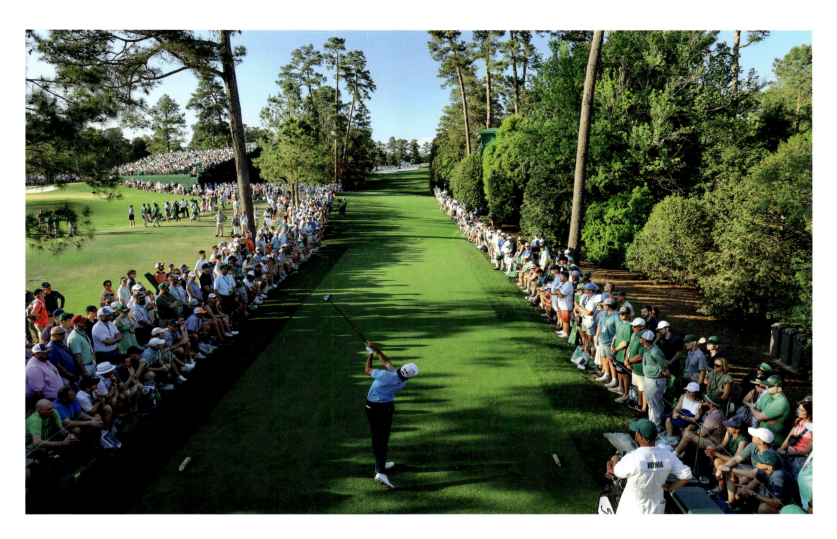

up) and Jordan Spieth was leading the tournament by two strokes when he returned a quadruple bogey in 2016.

'Azalea' is the last of the troublesome trio, just five yards longer than the 11th but clocking up as a par-5 and luring those wishing to make eagle to take on Rae's Creek. Hitting over the back can leave players in one of the many bunkers and will demand a very fine judgement of pace for the recovery shot — land your approach on the bank and you're in the stream.

Being the only major with a permanent venue, the drama that has unfolded over the closing holes has been seared into the consciousness of armchair golfers the world over. Many club golfers harbour a never-to-be-fulfilled dream of playing a round at Augusta. They should try the Augusta Country Club its southerly neighbour — it has azaleas, Georgia pines and you can enjoy a reckless moment by taking on Rae's Creek. It flows past the front of the par-5 8th green, just before it glides next door to intimidate golfers on the National's 12th hole.

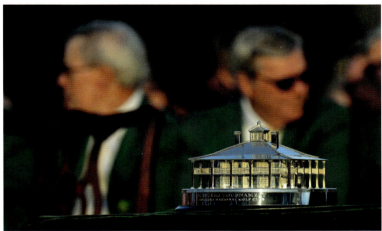

run, talk loudly or cheer when players make a mistake. And the tournament is all the better for it.

Accurate approach shots are more useful than prayers at Amen Corner which consists of the 11th, 12th and 13th holes. It is here the winding Rae's Creek makes its presence felt. The 505-yard, par-4 ,11th hole 'White Dogwood' features water guarding the front left of the green and many players will lay up short for a straightforward up-and-down rather than betting the farm and going for the flag.

The 12th is 'Golden Bell', a short par-3 with Rae's Creek in front and bunkers fore and aft. It is both beautiful and deadly, handing Tom Weiskopf a 13 in 1980 (though you suspect that after about the 8th stroke he will have given

ONE OF THE GREATEST COLLECTIONS OF MODERN GOLF COURSES, BANDON DUNES HAS DEVELOPED DISTINCT IDENTITIES FOR ITS SIX TRACKS

BANDON DUNES RESORT

BANDON, OREGON, USA

'Bandon Dunes is true to the spirit of Scotland's ancient links' is the sell-line for the resort on America's Pacific Northwest coast. We've heard that one before, but in the case of the most recent addition to the collection of fine courses on the Oregon shoreline, it is the perfect description.

Before getting into the reason why, it might be helpful to give a quick run-down of the genealogy of Bandon. The first course, Bandon Dunes, was designed by Scotsman David McLay Kidd, the son of a golf course superintendent who had spent his childhood summers roaming the dunes of Machrihanish. It opened in 1999 as a gentle introduction to the delights of links golf. The second course, Pacific Dunes (2001), was a Tom Doak design and golf reviewers immediately promoted it above its predecessor. Next up was Bandon Trails (2005) from Bill Coore and Ben Crenshaw. As the name suggests, it differs from the previous duo in that it heads inland, winding through dunes into meadows and forest land, with no ocean frontage.

Three top courses would seem enough for any resort already rated as one of the best in the world, but owners Mike Keiser and Phil Friedmann were far from done. Old Macdonald arrived in 2010 as a tribute to the Father of American golf course architecture, Charles Blair Macdonald, designer of the Chicago Golf Club and the National Golf Links on Long Island. Although again crafted by Doak it had a change of approach from Pacific Dunes, starting off inland, moving over the dunes, before opening out with great views of the Pacific and incorporating many 'ghost trees'. These dead, skeletal trees have been preserved in their leafless, barkless state, particularly near the 3rd hole 'Sahara'. They also appear as the course's logo on flagsticks.

Bandon continued the trend of releasing courses every few years like they were Bruce Springsteen albums. The fifth course, Bandon Preserve (2012) is a par-3 short course, which was followed by The Punchbowl in 2014. This was more like an EP, an elaborate 100,000-square-foot, 18-hole putting course designed by Doak and Urbina to match St Andrews' historic Ladies Putting Club which is also known as 'Himalayas'.

And then we come to the Sheep Ranch.

The owners had an inviting mile-long stretch of coast, the site of a defunct wind farm from the 1970s, which had closed because the turbines couldn't handle the gusts of wind ripping onshore. It was 140 acres in size (for comparison the modern Muirfield is 167 acres) and initially viewed as too small for an 18-hole course. Nevertheless back in 2001 when Tom Doak was hanging out in Oregon to supervise Pacific Dunes he was asked to create 13 greens on the property with the instruction that each green could be approached from any angle.

After construction finished, the 13-hole 'course' was a true reflection of seventeenth- and eighteenth-century Scottish golf, with no bunkers, no specific routing, no irrigation on the greens, but most likely, better mowers.

Golfers had a suggested route, but if they wanted, they could pick their own sequence of holes — typically the person with the honour chose the next green to aim at. There was no altercations between players criss-crossing between greens as this 'secret' course was limited to two groups a day. It cost $100 per player, but you had to be in the know to ask about it.

Eventually, with the insatiable desire to add more courses, the owners finally found a way of eking Sheep Ranch out to 6,636 yards over 18 holes, which included nine glorious greens along the Pacific. There is nothing like saving the best till last. When it opened in 2020 it was considered the best of all six courses. More than that, Bandon has been able to create distinctive identities for each of their designs, making it one of the ultimate destinations for golfers who appreciate a sea breeze.

Opposite The Lodge at Bandon Dunes viewed beyond the 13th green of Bandon Preserve, the par-3 course designed by Bill Coore and Ben Crenshaw that sits between Bandon Trails and Bandon Dunes courses.

Above A view from behind the green on the par-4, 17th hole of the Sheep Ranch course.

Right The 'Ghost Tree' logo used on pin flags of the Old Macdonald course designed by Tom Doak and Jim Urbina.

ONE OF THE TOUGHEST COURSES ON THE EAST COAST, AMATEUR PLAYERS ARE ADVISED TO CONSIDER IF IT'S WORTH THE STRESS...

BETHPAGE BLACK

FARMINGDALE, NEW YORK, USA·

For skiers, the order of difficulty on pistes is green, blue, red, black with black the toughest test, the steepest slopes, the nastiest moguls. It's fitting that at Bethpage Black there is a celebrated warning sign. 'WARNING The Black Course Is An Extremely Difficult Course Which We Recommend Only For Highly Skilled Golfers'. Not the kind of place to go off-piste.

Bethpage State Park is located in suburban Long Island, not so far from New York City. Tough golfing challenge + close to urban area = perfect Ryder Cup venue.

There are five courses in all to try at this publicly owned facility and like the skiing hierarchy, the simplest is green, moving through yellow, blue and red to black.

Compared to some of the old money courses of the East Coast, Bethpage was a late arrival. St Andrews at Hastings-on-the-Hudson has been there since 1888, and it was not until the Depression era that the local authority stepped in and purchased the Lenox Hills Country Club at Farmingdale complete with its golf course.

Bethpage State Park was developed as part of the WPA plan to boost jobs, and the original country club golf course from 1923 became the Green Course. By 1936, three more courses designed by A.W. Tillinghast of the 'Philadelphia School' were opened (Blue, Red and Black) with the fifth (Yellow) only arriving in 1958.

Although Bethpage Black had been punishing the local scratch golfers for some time, it was in 2002 and the visit of the US Open that really put Tillinghast's great work on the map. It was the first time the tournament had been hosted by a publicly owned course — 'The People's Open' — and rumours in the media abounded that the professionals were going to take it apart. This, of course, was in the era of Tiger domination and as it turned out, Tiger won. He was the only player under par at –3. Seven years later the US Open returned and this time Bethpage Black let its defences down and five players finished under par.

It is viewed as a 7,468-yard brute, and 6,700 yards from the middle tees, with the old adage that players will need every club in the bag. Provided you don't have a 2-iron in the bag — or as Lee Trevino calls it, his lightning protection — "because even God couldn't hit a 2-iron".

CHAMBERS BAY BECAME THE FIRST COURSE IN THE PACIFIC NORTHWEST TO HOST THE US OPEN

CHAMBERS BAY

CHAMBERS CREEK, WASHINGTON, USA

Hosting the US Open was a remarkable result for a golf course without the storied past of a Pebble Beach, an Oakmont or a Shinnecock Hills. What had been the site of a gravel mine, a lumber mill and a rail yard, was bought by Pierce County in 1992 and left for a decade to become the haunt of off-road four-wheelers and dirt-bikers.

When a top golf course was suggested by an enterprising county executive, the plan to spend $20m of public money on... yes, golf... naturally went down like a stone in Puget Sound in some quarters. It was intended to be the Pacific Northwest's equivalent to Torrey Pines, a public course capable of hosting major championships. To ensure maximum bang for the public buck the project leaders considered proposals from more than 50 leading golf architect design companies, including Phil Mickelson and Jack Nicklaus. Robert Trent Jones, Jr. got the commission, largely thanks to his work on the Greenback and Great Blue courses in north Portland.

With the climate of Washington State similar to that of the British Isles, the plan was to create a landscape that echoed the dunes of Oregon and build a Scottish links-style course on it. The site already had Royal Troon's railroad as an Out of Bounds, the former Northern Pacific Railway's main line ran along the shoreline. During construction, the earth-movers shifted around 1.4 million cubic yards of earth and sand to sculpt the landscape into the duneland of the old country — the fact that the site still had permits to operate as a working mine kept costs lower.

True to the spirit of links golf, when it opened in 2007 there was only one tree on the whole course, the Lone Fir behind the 15th green — and even then it was so far back it didn't come into play. The course likes to bill itself as 'America's answer to St Andrews' but whoever started that sales pitch hasn't been to Fife.

Chambers Bay has interesting industrial relics from the past dotted around the course, a reminder of twentieth century use — St Andrews has 300-year-old stone walls. There is 600 feet (183m) of elevation across the course and fantastic views across Puget Sound at Chambers Bay – players barely catch a glimpse of the sea on the Old Course

Above There are many vestiges of the site's former industrial use across the course that have been left in place.

Opposite top Chambers Bay's lone fir tree overlooks the par-3, 15th green and the 16th tee.

Opposite bottom Hunter Mahan drives from the 16th tee as a heavily loaded goods train passes by during the 2015 US Open.

because it is so flat. There is the Swilcan Burn at St Andrews, there are no water hazards at Chambers Bay. The routing of the Old Course is a traditional out-and-back, at Chambers Bay the first nine holes circle back to the clubhouse, so it's easy enough to start off from the first or the 10th tee. And it's Troon that has the railroad bordering the course.

The Pacific Northwest has impressive rainfall figures, but the Chambers Bay greens remain firm, while the fairways are generous and the rough surprisingly light. There was criticism after the 2015 US Open about the quality of the greens — though not from Jordan Spieth who was probably the world's best putter at the time and won with a superlative 3-wood from 285 yards out on the final hole, leaving him 15 feet from the pin. There is now a plaque in the fairway to mark the spot.

To iron out the inconsistency the pros experienced, the grass variety on the greens was switched from fescue to poa annua and Chambers Bay has been able to attract further high-profile tournaments including the US Junior Amateur Championship (2027) as well as the return of the US Amateur Championship in 2033. However with the US rota already fixed till 2051, there is no place for Chambers Bay for the decades to come.

For the amateur it remains an inviting test. There are five sets of tees available, giving a total yardage of 5,250 to 7,585 yards, all of which must be walked. Only a medical exemption will get you a cart, so be prepared to walk the 14,000 steps up, down and across this natural amphitheatre. The magnificent views across Puget Sound are ample reward — and for trainspotting golfers, with a strong interest in industrial history who love a sea view. Well, this place is heaven.

Opposite An authentic links course with an authentic, if misplaced, windmill. C.B. Macdonald's classic course has hosted the Walker Cup in its time.

Above The 17th is surrounded by sand, but it has an open approach that allows for a finely-judged run-up.

LEARNING FROM OLD TOM MORRIS, CHARLES MACDONALD SET ABOUT CREATING COURSES IN THE NEW WORLD

NATIONAL GOLF LINKS OF AMERICA
SOUTHAMPTON, NEW YORK, USA

The National Golf Links of America is easily identifiable, it's the one with the windmill. It was created by the Father of American Golf Architecture, C.B. Macdonald, who built his course on the rolling landscape of Long Island, right next to Shinnecock Hills.

Born in Canada, Macdonald spent the 1870s at St Andrews University, playing golf on the Old Course with both Old and Young Tom Morris. When he returned to Chicago in 1874, with no courses to play, his enthusiasm for the game dwindled. Rekindled in the 1890s, he laid out the very first 18-hole course in America in 1893 — up until then they had all been nine- or twelve-hole courses.

In the earliest US clubs, little attention was paid to the layout — greens were usually square, but having played golf in Scotland, Macdonald knew he could build something special, perhaps the greatest golf course in America. Starting in 1902 he made five summer trips to sketch out the holes he most admired on British courses and then handed his plans to Seth Raynor, a local civil engineer. Macdonald was a stockbroker by trade.

His borrowed holes included 'Sahara' from Royal St George's, 'Alps' from Prestwick, 'Redan' the par-3 from North Berwick, the 'Road' hole and 'High(in)' from St Andrews and, for good measure, a par-4 from Sunningdale. The greens were generous like those of the Old Course. When it opened in 1909 it produced a sensational response from American golfers.

But the distinguishing feature on the course is not of the golfing variety, the 'Greatest Hits' of British golf. It's a windmill located between the 2nd and 16th holes. A member of this exclusive club once remarked that a windmill would make a nice addition to the course. Macdonald's reaction is unrecorded, but he bought one when he was next in Europe and sent the member the bill.

OAKMONT IS FAMOUS FOR ITS BEAUTIFULLY MAINTAINED BUNKERS, BUT ALSO ITS SURREPTITIOUS DISPOSAL OF TREES...

OAKMONT

PLUM, PENNSYLVANIA, USA

Golf architect Alister MacKenzie once said: 'A good golf course is like good music. It does not necessarily appeal the first time one plays it.' Oakmont may well fit that description — golfers who have played it over the years find it tough at first, appreciate it second and then fall in love.

Around the turn of the nineteenth century Henry Fownes' mission was to create a links-style course on farmland on the outskirts of Pittsburgh in Western Pennsylvania. Although the land bordered the Allegheny River, it was a long way from the sea. There would be no beachside opening drives or greens perched on rocky cliffs or burns snaking to the ocean, in fact no water hazards at all. Oakmont is the home of bunkers — but what bunkers.

After a year's construction work, the course was open for play in 1903. By 1927 it was on the US Open rota and has hosted the tournament ten times in total, the latest in 2025.

Fownes started off with around 200 bunkers and his son, William Fownes added more till the number approached 300 — although that number has since been reduced. Part of that work involved the amalgamation of a number of small

Above The Oakmont clubhouse where mass arboricide was planned — but all with the very best of intentions.

Right Ridging of bunker sand adds an extra dimension to escaping traps around the course, one of the US Open's most visited venues.

Opposite The famous 'Church Pews' bunker. Given the number of high profile tournaments held at Oakmont, the great and the good of world golf have all prayed for a favourable outcome from this hazard.

bunkers between the 3rd and 4th fairways to make the behemoth of bunkers known as Church Pews. At first there were eight grass berms dividing this most iconic of course hazards, but the congregation has expanded and now there are 12. Over the years the grass length on top of the berms has varied from fully mown to uncut rough, but it is the ball's resting place in relation to the lip of the grass that will most affect the next shot.

It is an unusual championship course in that it is bisected by the Pennsylvania Turnpike. The intrusion of transport was right there from the start. The golf course was constructed around the Allegheny Valley branch of the Pennsylvania Railroad which had run across the site since the late

nineteenth century. With the line pulled up, the turnpike followed its routing in the 1940s.

One of the most dramatic intrigues that has faced the club has been the secret removal of trees from the course. Fownes had intended the course to be open and links-like, in other words, not like a country park. He clearly achieved that because a visiting Bobby Jones commented that a golfer standing at the rear of the clubhouse at Oakmont could look out over the course and see 17 of the 18 flagsticks.

It was still like that in 1962 when influential golf writer Herbert Warren Wind (the man who coined the phrase 'Amen Corner' at Augusta) arrived to cover the US Open

and described it as 'that ugly, old brute'. Long-time club president Fred Brand Jr. took offence and set about a makeover that involved the planting of 3,500 trees around the course. In time, the pin oaks, flowering cherries and blue spruce (not native to that area of Western Pennsylvania) grew up, shading and dividing out the fairways. By the late 1980s Oakmont was just another parkland course, albeit one with memorable bunkers.

Many thought it should return to Fownes' original vision. Starting in the 1990s, grounds chairman Banks Smith devised a plan for the clandestine removal of the latterly introduced trees. In an operation worthy of a TV drama, a crew of 12 would set out to remove unsuspecting trees under the cover of darkness. Work began at 4.30 a.m. using the illumination of cart headlights, with tarpaulins stretched across the ground to catch sawdust and chippings. Once removed, the logs were stored away from sight behind the clubhouse, stumps were ground down and turf placed over the site of the old trunk. Two sweepers had the job of tidying up leaves. As maintenance staff rarely mix with club members in the bar, a code of *omerta* was unnecessary.

The plot came unstuck when a member noticed that a group of 13 trees between the 12th and 13th holes had dwindled to three. From that point on, there was open debate in the club between those who wanted to retain the remaining trees and those who wanted the course as it was intended. The fact that these weren't ancient specimens, were non-native to that part of Pennsylvania and their absence allowed a great improvement in the quality of the fairway turf won the argument. Further removal also added room for more grandstands during tournaments.

When golfers familiar with 1994 US Open footage turned up to play the course in 2007 they were staggered by the transformation. However, everyone is on board with the new treeless Oakmont, and there is no going back to parkland — even if the club logo *is* a squirrel holding a golf ball...

PINEHURST HAS A STATUE, BUT TIGER WOODS HAS HELPED CREATE A PLAYABLE LEGACY TO THE MOST BELOVED OF GOLFERS

PAYNE'S VALLEY

RIDGEDALE, MISSOURI, USA

Payne's Valley was the third 18-hole course to be added at Big Cedar Lodge when it opened in 2020. Having employed Tom Fazio and Coore & Crenshaw for the first two courses, owner Johnny Morris managed to snag Tiger Woods' company, TGR, for his first collaboration in public course design for the third.

The name of the course is significant. It's a tribute to the late great Payne Stewart who grew up in Springfield, Missouri, 50 miles to the north.

The course is a par-72 of 7,370 yards with immaculate, cold-tolerant zoysia fairways and bentgrass greens lining the rehabilitated limestone quarry.

There are some standout holes, including a peninsula green on the par-3, 5th (to all intents and purposes an island hole), water surrounding the green on the par-3, 10th, and a par-5 18th that demands a drive across water, playing to a green below the enormous rock face, with water behind.

There is the additional Johnny Morris 19th sitting at the base of the cliff face. This is a true island hole that can be played as a detour on the way back to the clubhouse, which sits at a commanding height above the course.

To open the course Tiger invited along Justin Thomas, Rory McIlroy and Justin Rose for a fun game along with Gary Player and Jack Nicklaus who had both designed smaller courses at the resort. Justin Rose recalled an early encounter with Payne Stewart at an Open Championship. "I was with a group of kids hoping to get a golf ball from one of the pros," said Rose. "Payne pointed to me, threw me a ball… from that moment on I was always rooting for Payne."

Son Aaron Stewart joined the major winners for the opening round of what was a joyous occasion for golf.

Above The long, par-3, 17th hole at Pebble Beach with the 18th tee on the promontory beyond.

THERE ARE MANY GREAT GOLF COURSES ALONG MONTEREY'S 17-MILE DRIVE, BUT PEBBLE BEACH IS THE MOST CELEBRATED

PEBBLE BEACH

MONTEREY PENINSULA, CALIFORNIA, USA

One might say that the Monterey Peninsula is the East Lothian of California. The Scottish district to the east of Edinburgh has Musselburgh, Royal Musselburgh, Levenhall, Gullane, Muirfield, Renaissance, Archerfield and North Berwick, all jostling for position along the coastline, or not far inland. Monterey has a host of world-class golf courses too, of which Pebble Beach is the most famous.

Over the years it has received every accolade the game can throw at it. Master golf architect Robert Trent Jones Sr. adored it: 'The first time I ever saw Pebble Beach, I thought I had died and gone to heaven. It's one of the most beautiful places on Earth. It's the unrivalled counterpart to

Pine Valley among our oceanside courses. I say "oceanside" and not "seaside," because seaside has come to imply low-lying linksland, and Pebble Beach is quite the reverse. It is routed along the craggy headlands that drop abruptly into Carmel Bay.'

Jack Nicklaus has been fulsome with his praise, too. 'If I had only one more round to play, I would choose to play it at Pebble Beach. I've loved this course from the first time I saw it.'

Pebble Beach links course was built to be part of a hotel resort complex. As early as 1880 Southern Pacific Railroad had invested in the Del Monte Hotel which received railroad tourists travelling to see the splendours of Pacific Grove and Monterrey. The hotel devised a carriage route, the renowned 17-Mile Drive, to take visitors for an invigorating jaunt through the peninsula.

Work on the course did not start in earnest until the twentieth century, with champion amateur golfers Jack Neville and Douglas Grant given the task of creating a course by developer Samuel F.B. Morse. They had never designed a course before, but were blessed with the most exquisite piece of real estate for their first attempt. Speaking to the *San Francisco Chronicle* in later years Neville underplayed their achievement. 'It was all there in plain sight. Very little clearing was necessary. The big thing, naturally, was to get as many holes as possible along the bay. It took a little imagination, but not much. Years before

Opposite top The pocket-sized green on the par-3, 5th hole with the 6th hole behind.

Opposite bottom A view from behind the green on the par-4, 8th hole.

Above Looking back from behind the green on the par-5, 18th hole, where tournaments, have been won or lost — or tied, as in 1984 when a lucky bounce off the rocks helped Hale Irwin make a birdie and then win the Bing Crosby (now the AT&T) playoff.

it was built, I could see this place as a golf links. Nature had intended it to be nothing else. All we did was cut away a few trees, install a few sprinklers, and sow a little seed.' Old Tom Morris would have loved that modest candour.

Tom Fazio believes it to be a 'masterpiece', but other golf architects have contributed to the picture over the years. H. Chandler Egan, Alister MacKenzie, Robert Hunter have all left their touches and Jack Nicklaus helped create the new 5th hole in 1998. Fazio himself has contributed work, but was mindful of altering too much. 'The challenge is to make improvements while preserving the character and tradition that make it one of the greatest courses in the world.'

Nobody wants to be the golfing equivalent of Cecilia Giménez, the amateur art restorer in Spain who gained worldwide fame with her botched restoration of Elías García Martínez's fresco of Jesus, turning it into what one visitor described as 'a blurry potato'.

Unlike nearby Cypress Point, which is a private club and inaccessible to the average player, Pebble Beach is a public course open to those with a sufficiently large bank balance. As such, in 2001, it became the first public course to be selected by the mighty *Golf Digest* as the No.1 Golf Course in America. And they have played Cypress Point.

Although the inland holes may lack charisma, the stretch from the 7th to the 10th leaves golfers breathless. The most familiar green at Pebble Beach is that of the short 7th hole, a par-3 surrounded by bunkers and if the weather is right, pounding Pacific surf of which a zillion photographs have been published.

The 18th hole that curves round the bay to the clubhouse is one of the great closing par-5s of world golf. Like at the 7th, during blustery tournament play the green keepers need to be on standby to squeegee the greens when things get wet, especially during the annual AT&T National Pro-Am scheduled in the early months of the year.

What makes Pebble Beach stand above so many other courses is that it combines beauty with a stern golfing challenge. The US Open organizers pride themselves at setting up courses which demand the maximum concentration and Pebble Beach has hosted the event six times, with a seventh planned for 2027. At the 2000 US Open, played at Pebble Beach, Tiger Woods won by a jaw-dropping 15 shots, the biggest margin of victory at any major golf tournament.

Is it any wonder that golfers are prepared to pay $700 for a round of golf to walk in the footsteps of giants...?

PINEHURST WITH ITS NINE COURSES HAS BECOME A MECCA FOR GOLFERS, BUT NONE IS MORE PRESTIGIOUS THAN THE CENTURY-OLD No.2

PINEHURST No.2

PINEHURST, NORTH CAROLINA, USA

Pinehurst is the result of the Great American Dream, that of a 16-year-old drugstore apprentice who rose to become a great entrepreneur. James Walker Tufts was the inventor of the Arctic Soda Fountain. He became a rich man and latterly a philanthropist. In 1895 he bought 5,500 acres in North Carolina with the intention of building 'a health resort for people of modest means'. Originally dubbed 'Tuftstown', Tufts hired the company of Central Park landscape architect Frederick Law Olmsted to design the village which would eventually become Pinehurst.

The first golf course was laid out in 1897–98. The No.1 course, complete with its square greens, started the numerical sequence for which Pinehurst tracks are still known. Although No.1 hosted the prestigious United North and South Amateur Championship early on, it was the No.2 course that put it on the map.

In 1900, Donald Ross was appointed as golf professional at Pinehurst. A native of Dornoch in Scotland, Ross was the ultimate golfing polymath. He had been apprenticed under Old Tom Morris at St Andrews, was a club maker, a greenkeeper and a talented golfer to boot. Ross finished fifth in the 1903 US Open at Baltusrol and won the princely sum of £5 by finishing eighth in the 1910 Open Championship at St Andrews. But it was golf course design at which he really excelled, working on 400 in his lifetime.

His No.2 course of 1907 was immediately adjudged as a championship-standard 18 holes. The elevated greens he introduced to the United States were modelled on those he'd built at Royal Dornoch, sometimes described as 'domed' or 'turtle-back'.

Johnny Miller likened them to putting on top of a VW beetle, and when they ran fast, as in the 2024 US Open,

Above An aerial view of the Pinehurst Resort clubhouse along with The Cradle par-3 course. Pinehurst hosted the 2024 US Open Championship.

Right When squirrels sense danger they may flatten themselves against the ground to avoid casting a shadow and remain inconspicuous. It hasn't worked for this squirrel at Pinehurst.

Opposite top Pinehurst has nine courses named in sequence of construction, but only two, Nos.2 and 3, remain attributed to Donald Ross. This is the par-3, 6th hole on No.2.

Opposite bottom The par-3, 9th hole. Even though Donald Ross was the most prolific of golf architects, he would return to tinker with his courses until his death – at Pinehurst – in 1948.

it was tough to score low. Only eight players finished the most recent Pinehurst Open under par, and the world's No.1 golfer, Scottie Scheffler at two over par, had to settle for a tie for 41st.

Pinehurst No.2, as envisioned by Ross, was a sandhills course without need of rough, but in 1974 Robert Trent Jones revised the course, introducing areas of Bermuda grass. For purists, it was unwelcome meddling. Thanks to the existence of aerial photos from the 1930s, Bill Coore and Ben Crenshaw were able to undertake a $2.5 million restoration to the original Donald J. design, reshaping the fairways and stripping out the rough to return it to scrub and hardpan sand.

Payne Stewart won a memorable US Open at Pinehurst in 1999, holing an 18-foot putt on the final green to defeat Phil Mickelson. It was Stewart's last major before his untimely death four months later and the club have honoured him with a fine statue in his winning pose. The 2014 event was another standout tournament at No.2 with Germany's Martin Kaymer streaking away from the field by eight shots. Ten years later there was drama in the final two holes when Rory McIlroy's missed short putts left the door open for Bryson deChambeau.

As a vote of confidence to the challenge of Pinehurst's 'Old Course', the US Open will be returning in 2029, 2035, 2041 and 2047.

Above Tom Watson's favourite hole the twin-greened, short par-4, 8th. There are also alternative greens on the 9th. One hole further on, at the 10th, there is a small deep bunker, that *Golf Digest* eloquently notes, 'has a deep gravitational pull' and a Satanic nickname to boot.

Right A side view of the 7th green. To have reached here golfers must have crossed 'Hell's Half Acre' on a par-5 that is 636 yards from the back tee.

NO OTHER COURSE HAS THE REPUTATION OF PINE VALLEY AS THE ULTIMATE TEST OF GOLFING SKILLS

PINE VALLEY

PINE HILL, NEW JERSEY, USA

Pine Valley is unique in its place amongst top American golf courses. It does not have the scintillating views of courses in the high mountains, or a raging ocean by its side, or the familiarity of being regularly viewed on televised tournaments. What it has is a collection of holes that present golfers with such a variety of challenges that the sum is far greater than its parts.

The great architect Robert Trent Jones Sr. wrote that, 'it possesses more classic holes than any other course in the world – ten of the eighteen. Of the remaining holes, five are outstanding, two are good, and one, the 12th, is ordinary, which, at Pine Valley, is tantamount to being a misfit.'

It can be a punishing course, 'a beautiful monster' that has to be learned. Pine Valley members took a delight in challenging new arrivals at the club to break 80 on their first visit, a serious bet that the young Arnold Palmer took up in 1954, just before he turned professional. Arnie returned a 68 and won a considerable sum of money, much to wife Winnie's relief. In 1958 the reputation of Pine Valley as the nation's greatest golfing test was highlighted on the cover of *Sports Illustrated* magazine, which posed the question: 'World's Most Demanding Golf Course?'. What was true then is true now.

The course was founded in 1913 by a group of enthusiastic amateur golfers from Philadelphia led by hotelier George Crump. They purchased an area of sandy scrub pineland in southern New Jersey, and Crump took on the role of course designer. He set himself a tough manifesto for what his holes should be: no hole should be laid out parallel to the next; only two consecutive holes could head in the same direction; and players' should not be able to see any hole other than the one they were playing

Harry Colt was brought in to advise Crump on the routing and with his seal of approval went full steam-winch ahead, dragging out 22,000 tree stumps, draining marshland and assembling 14 playable holes by 1916. Some viewed it as a 'Crump's folly', just as buying Alaska had been deemed 'William Seward's folly', but both single-minded individuals struck gold.

Crump died in 1918 and never got to see his vision fully realized. The course was completed in 1919 and with the input of other architects has maintained an extraordinarily high bar. Cypress Point is an exclusive club, impossible to play, but then there's Pebble Beach nearby and other courses on the Monterey Peninsula. There's only one Pine Valley.

TAKE A DEEP BREATH AND LAUNCH A TEE-SHOT — THIS COURSE IN MONTANA IS WHERE YOU CAN GO BIG

THE RESERVE AT MOONLIGHT BASIN

BIG SKY RESORT, MONTANA, USA

Simply put, The Reserve at Moonlight Basin is breathtaking. In both senses of the word. It's situated high up in Montana, north of Yellowstone, amid the Spanish Peaks. At 7,500 feet of altitude, the course runs to an enormous length, 8,000 yards from the back tees, but at that kind of elevation the ball travels so much further, reputedly 14% further.

Indeed one of the factors of a round at The Reserve is working out exactly how far your ball is going to roll, particularly on the downhill slopes, of which there are many. Most golfers might tremble at a scorecard with a 777-yard par-5 on it, but the view from the 17th tee reassures you that it is downhill all the way. Add some ski-pulls to the side and you could easily imagine it as a ski run in winter.

Jack Nicklaus has designed a course that evokes awe and wonder. Tom Doak had already created a great Montana course with his Rock Creek Cattle Company, but to use the Spinal Tap analogy, this has cranked it up to 12 on the dial.

There may well be a hike between greens and the following tee, but that only heightens the sense of anticipation as to what the next tee will reveal. And with thin oxygen and many elevation changes, this is not a course intended to delight walking golfers.

Were it possible to bring Old Tom Morris here to show him what Jack has done with 'the Almighty Maun's' creation he would scarcely believe how far golf design has come. One reviewer commented that the final hole was a disappointment. Which may or may not be true, but it is like saying that da Vinci could have made the *Mona Lisa* a little better by adding a bit more detail on the sleeves.

Above Looking towards the par-4, 7th green and its barrage of interlocking bunkers.

Opposite top Riviera's Spanish Colonial-style clubhouse, set up for the Genesis Invitational in 2024.

Opposite bottom The greenkeeper uses a collar mower around the famous 6th green bunker.

FOUNDED IN THE 1920S, THE 18 HOLES COST AN EYE-WATERING SUM TO BUILD, BUT RAISED THE BAR ON COURSE DESIGN

RIVIERA COUNTRY CLUB
LOS ANGELES, CALIFORNIA, USA

The Riviera Club at Pacific Pallisades, on the northern edge of Los Angeles, was founded during the Golden Age of Hollywood. In the days before earth moving became easy, George C. Thomas spent a fortune ($250,000 — three times the normal budget for a golf course in that era) rearranging the landscape for what would surely become a glamorous playground for the stars of the silver screen. Indeed, after waiting 18 months for the course to be completed in 1927, Douglas Fairbanks and Charlie Chaplin became enthusiastic members, along with Harold Lloyd and W.C. Fields.

Today, the 18 holes have been much altered, but the routing is ostensibly the same. The course sets off from a high first tee from an elegant clubhouse built in Spanish Colonial Revival style. Then it's down into the flat valley floor uninterrupted by watercourses, save for a dry outwash or *barranca* before returning to the 18th and a climb back up to the clubhouse.

It's one of the many courses whose supporters maintain: there isn't a weak hole in the 18, but 'Riv', as it can be called, has a unique feature. The par-3, 6th hole has a bunker in the middle of what is a very large green. Players may use any club in their bag, so if the flagstick is left, the ball is right and the bunker is in between, it is quite legitimate for players to chip over it from the putting surface. Which is what Phil Mickelson has done on at least two occasions — when the Riviera has hosted the Genesis Invitational — and despite leaving divots on the 6th green, Mickelson continues to be invited back.

However, only the pros are allowed to do it. There is a note on the scorecard that stipulates amateur players must use putters. When the Olympics returns to Los Angeles in 2028, Riviera will be hosting the golf. Let's hope that they're all professionals to avoid any unpleasantness on the 6th.

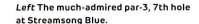
Left **The much-admired par-3, 7th hole at Streamsong Blue.**

ONE OF THE GREATEST CREATIVE RE-USES OF AN INDUSTRIAL SITE, STREAMSONG KEEPS ON ADDING COURSES TO ITS REPERTOIRE

STREAMSONG BLUE

BOWLING GREEN, FLORIDA, USA

Planning a major golf resort on the site of an old phosphorous strip mine, doesn't sound like the greatest of ideas, but the creators of Streamsong in Florida have pulled it off. You can check any assumptions about 'Florida golf' right here — the initial two courses immediately defied the stereotype.

Architects Coore & Crenshaw and Tom Doak were given a course each and collaborated on the best way to route the 36 holes. Doak's blue course sticks to the centre of the site, with more carries over water and a gigantic raised first tee not unlike the 9th hole at Cruden Bay. Coore & Crenshaw's course sticks to the periphery of the property, but cuts inside from the 14th hole home.

Tom Doak welcomed the topography that the site presented: 'The variety of contours created by the mining process is unique for a project in Florida.' Indeed, the mining engineers had inadvertently created a dunes-like appearance with all the quirky humps and hollows one might expect on the west coast of Ireland.

The fairways of Blue and Red are resort fairways, not aimed at frightening away the tourist dollar but there are still tricky contoured greens that love a curling putt. Most featured of all is the par-3, 7th hole on the Blue course, a 200-yard blow from the back tees over water to a green nestled at the bottom of a hummocky pocket of land and accessed by a bridge to the left.

After the success of Red and Blue, Streamsong Black from Gil Hanse was added in 2017 to make it 54 holes and, with an eye to what resorts like Bandon Dunes are doing, redialled Coore & Crenshaw's number. Bill and Ben were asked for a version of the Edinburgh Ladies Putting Club along with the most imaginative par-3 course they could fashion. The Chain (2023) certainly lives up to that brief.

HOME OF THE INCREASINGLY RARE TORREY PINE, THE BENEFICIARY OF THE COAST'S FREQUENT MARINE FOGS

TORREY PINES

LA JOLLA, CALIFORNIA, USA

There are two courses at Torrey Pines — the South course is the long and challenging championship course — and the North course is for those who want to say they've played at Torrey Pines. Actually, the rough on both courses is said to be punishing, but for those who like a scenic golf round, the North is better. The South has the ultimate cachet.

Torrey Pines is to be found perched on the coastal cliffs overlooking the Pacific Ocean, just south of Torrey Pines State Reserve and north of La Jolla cove on the outskirts of San Diego. The course is named after the Torrey pine, a rare and endangered tree that is only found on a coastal stretch of San Diego County and on Santa Rosa Island. It's believed that coastal fog during spring and summer gives them just enough moisture to supplement the low winter rainfall.

Like Bethpage on Long Island, it's a municipally owned facility and not long in the making. It was opened in 1957 on the site of a former World War II military installation. Local golfing hero Billy Casper tinkered with the layout of the South Course in the 1970s, but it was Rees Jones who completely rejuvenated it in 2001 at a cost of $3.5 million. Jones moved four greens, increased the number of bunkers (still only 54, less than the number on a single hole at Whistling Straits), and took the championship yardage out to 7,607 yards.

Apart from occasionally hosting the US Open (2008, won by Tiger Woods, 2021, won by Jon Rahm), it is a regular destination for the high-ranking PGA Farmers Insurance Open at the start of the Tour season. As a nod to the consistent quality of all 36 holes, both North and South courses are used for the first two rounds before play switches to the South course for the final two rounds.

Along with a rare pine species, nature lovers out on the course can spot coyote, bobcats, raccoons, mule deer, red-tail hawks, great blue herons, snow egrets, but more likely paragliders, which hang above the cliffs using the coastal thermals.

THE PGA CREATED THE FIRST 'STADIUM GOLF COURSE', CONVERTING SWAMP LAND INTO PREMIUM GOLFING REAL ESTATE

TPC SAWGRASS

PONTE VEDRA, FLORIDA, USA

The Tournament Players Club (TPC) at Sawgrass owes a lot of its success to a single hole that was built accidentally. Sited on Florida swampland and opened in 1980, the course had been a challenge to architects Pete and Alice Dye. As they excavated around the site they discovered a layer of sugar sand underneath the mud which could be used around the course. The mud was needed to create earth mounds for spectator viewing, as this was a PGA-commissioned course, a place to host the Players' Championship.

Originally the 17th hole had been a conventional short hole with a pond to the side to catch errant shots, very much like the 17th at Harbour Town. But as more and more mud was required, the pond was getting larger. Alice Dye then suggested it become an island green, giving them a lot more mud and sand to play with, while making it a real signature hole. At 137 yards Pete thought it would be too easy and wanted to angle it away from the tee. With rock hard greens Alice thought it would be tough enough as it was. Asked what he thought about the early course Jack Nicklaus replied, 'I've never been very good at stopping a 5-iron on the hood of a car.'

Despite early criticism, TPC Sawgrass has evolved into a likeable and challenging course, and the TPC concept rolled out multiple times across the United States. The accidental 17th has become one of the most copied holes in new courses around the world, especially in cultures where betting is a frequent part of a round of golf. An island hole gives an unequivocal outcome — between the quick and the out-of-pocket.

IT'S HARD TO COUNT THE BUNKERS AT THIS EXACTING EXAMINATION OF GOLFING SKILL, BUT MUCH EASIER TO FIND THEM...

WHISTLING STRAITS

SHEBOYGAN, WISCONSIN, USA

It is the hallmark of great golf course architects that they can produce golf courses with distinct appearances that confound identification as their handiwork — other than the testimony that it is a work of genius. Pete Dye's Harbour Town Links is all about the trees, Whistling Straits is all about the bunkers, a constellation of them.

The fact that they look such an integral and natural part of the landscape at Whistling Straits is validation to the subterfuge that has gone on here. The Kohler Company of Wisconsin had bought a great big lump of land on the shores of Lake Michigan previously occupied by Camp Haven, a military base set up to test anti-aircraft gunnery.

A 36-hole golf resort was welcomed by the community. The previous owner of the land had been a utilities company looking to set up the Haven Nuclear Power & Light Plant. When that got turned down, a companion site to the nearby Blackwolf Run golf complex seemed a much safer option.

Pete and Alice Dye set about transforming what was basically a piece of flat farmland at the edge of a lake to a rambling dunescape typified by the Ballybunion course (1893) on the wild west coast of County Kerry. What the site was lacking, was the great quantity of sand needed to fill the myriad bunkers that had been planned. It would be interesting to know if the project's driving force, Herb Kohler, ever said: "Erm, Pete... How many?" During the

Above **The 494-yard, par-4, 4th hole 'Glory', peppered with bunkers.**

Opposite top **It's a testing 249 yards from the back tee at the par-3, 17th hole, 'Pinched Nerve'.**

Opposite **bottom There's an interesting contrast between the pitted landscape of the 603-yard, par-5, 5th hole, 'Snake' and the flat, undeveloped countryside beyond.**

course of construction something like 13,000 truckloads of sand arrived to fill the 900+ bunkers.

In 2010 *Golf Digest's* Ron Whitten set about counting them all, a two-day endeavour that came up with a total of 967. Although since then the magazine has revised that figure up to 1,012 in their course review. Ron found the 8th as the most bunkered hole with 102, followed by the 18th with 96. The 12th and 14th had a paltry 18 each. When the course made its debut in 1998 one reviewer joked that there should be about 25 bunkers on the driving range: 'to give players a taste of what is to come.'

And what is to come is an arduous test for the professional golfer. Kohler wanted a championship-level course and Dye wanted to create a challenge where length off the tee wasn't everything. As Jason Lusk explained in an insightful 2021 Ryder Cup preview: 'Always interested in getting into the heads of the pros and thumbing his nose at their power, Dye constructed a layout of twists and turns, humps and hollows, sand and more sand. If pros could hit just about any target within sight, why not simply

hide those targets to mess with the heads of the best?'

That was certainly the case with the European team at the Ryder Cup that year as the US buried Pádraig Harrington's side 19–9. Mike O' Reilly, golf operations manager at companion club Blackwolf Run, which Dye had designed a decade earlier, is of the same opinion. 'I think he did an amazing job with the visual intimidation on any particular shot, then you get out to the space and say, it didn't really look like this from back at the tee box. Just some of those mind tricks that he plays — it looks very difficult, very visually intimidating.'

To make it even more authentic to the British Isles' ambiance a flock of Scottish blackface sheep are free to roam the property. Dye has also incorporated more bunker-bolstering railways sleepers as found at the Royal North Devon club in Westward Ho! and there are no golf carts. Whistling Straits is a walking course where players must hire a caddie for their round. Given the nature of the challenge presented, this is surely no bad thing.

A LUSH GOLFING OASIS IN THE NEVADA DESERT, RIGHT IN THE HEART OF THE ENTERTAINMENT CAPITAL OF THE WORLD

Above Despite its desert location, water is never far away at the super-compact Wynn Las Vegas course, with the two, bronze towers of Wynn and Encore dominating the skyline.

Opposite top Overlooked by a waterfall, the 448-yard, par-4, 18th hole is a suitable showstopper to finish a round in Vegas.

Opposite bottom Formula 1 driver Pierre Gasly tests his short game at the 2023 Netflix Cup.

WYNN LAS VEGAS

LAS VEGAS, NEVADA, USA

If Augusta National has become an iconic golf course thanks to its annual exposure on primetime sports television, then the golf course at Wynn Las Vegas may follow suit. The successful launch of the F1 Las Vegas Grand Prix in 2023 was accompanied by the Netflix Cup teaming F1 drivers with PGA Stars — and given their media and sponsor commitments, the likes of Lando Norris, Carlos Sainz and Pierre Gasly couldn't stray far from the pit lane. The Wynn Golf Club was perfect for the event.

It wasn't the first time the site had hosted a televised tournament. Steve Wynn bought the Desert Inn casino complete with its 18-hole golf course in 2000. Prior to that it had hosted many big money PGA events, including the Tournament of Champions from 1953 to 1966.

At first Wynn thought the land too valuable to leave as a golf course and some of the acreage was used to build the Wynn Resort, followed by Encore, but then he had a change of heart. In 2005 Tom Fazio was brought in to transform the ground into a lush oasis in the Nevada desert. The earth movers arrived to push around 400,000 cubic yards of earth — lakes and streams were added along with the kind of waterfall that is perfect for the supercharged excess of Vegas, but wrong in almost every other new golf course.

Fazio managed to incorporate 1,200 of the legacy trees from Desert Inn days and has added 7,000 more to create a challenging, tree-lined course set against the towering landmarks of downtown Vegas. True, it's an expensive round of golf, but factor in other extras for a round at the world's top courses and it doesn't seem excessive. Whether it can withstand the march of development in the world's capital of entertainment is another thing altogether.

ROYAL PORTRUSH

ROSAPENNA RESORT

BALLYLIFFIN
GOLF CLUB

ROYAL COUNTY
DOWN

BALLYBUNION OLD COURSE

WATERVILLE
GOLF CLUB

OLD HEAD
GOLF LINKS

IRELAND

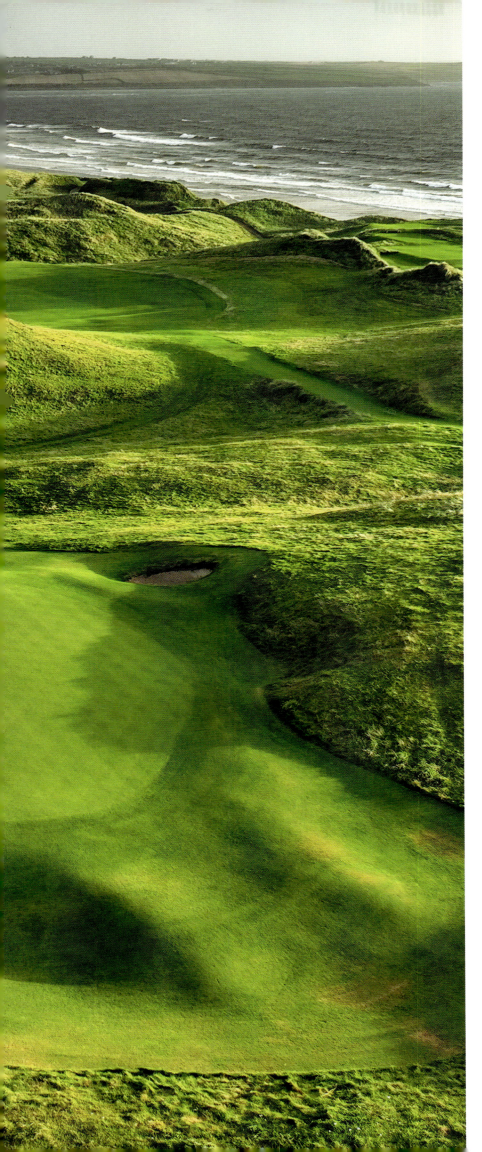

GOLF'S ELITE HAVE REGULARLY SUNG THE PRAISES OF THIS LINKS COURSE, LITTLE CHANGED SINCE THE NINETEENTH CENTURY

BALLYBUNION OLD COURSE

BALLYBUNION, COUNTY KERRY, IRELAND

To the north of Tralee on the Kerry coast is Ballybunion, a links course that many find hard to beat. Golf writer Herbert Warren Wind (the terror of Oakmont and the man who coined 'Amen Corner') wrote in the *New Yorker* in 1971: 'I found Ballybunion to be nothing less than the finest seaside links I have ever seen.' No slim praise indeed.

There are two courses at Ballybunion, the Old Course and the Cashen Course (1980), by Robert Trent Jones. The Cashen skirts along the coast to the south of the Old Course, right the way down to the mouth of the River Feale.

The Old Course had been there since 1893 and was revised ahead of the 1937 Irish Amateur Championship by eccentric English golf architect Tom Simpson. Simpson, who had laid out many courses in France including Deauville (with Henry Cotton), Hardelot and Fontainbleau, was fond of wearing a beret and cape and regarded himself as an artist. He arrived at the course in a chauffeur-driven Rolls Royce with glamorous assistant Molly Gourlay and the couple set out with a Fortnum & Mason's picnic basket to survey the course.

He declared that Ballybunion had 'terrain that surpasses any course we know for beauty', and that he did not need to revise much, the course only needed some 'finishing touches'. And it has remained so.

Despite limited media exposure, the course gained a trickle of well-travelled admirers in the 1970s — but interest exploded after Tom Watson won the Open at Royal Troon in 1982. Accepting the Claret Jug from the R&A he said: "Nobody can call himself a golfer until he has played at Ballybunion; you would think the game originated there!" That probably went down a treat at St Andrews. He later added that it was, "a course on which many golf architects should live and play before they build golf courses. I consider it a true test of golf."

A CLUB NURTURED FOR YEARS BY ITS LOCAL MEMBERS HAS NOW GAINED AN INTERNATIONAL REPUTATION

BALLYLIFFIN GOLF CLUB

BALLYLIFFIN, COUNTY DONEGAL, IRELAND

For golfers who listen to the Shipping Forecast, there is a daily update on the weather you can expect at Ballyliffin Golf Club. It lies very close to the northern tip of the Irish mainland, near the weather station at Malin Head, and its coastal waters include the island of Glashedy, the translation from gaelic means 'the island of the green cloak', which is a description that could easily be applied to the fairways at Ballyliffin.

Situated on the tip of the Inishowen Peninsula in Donegal it consists of the Old Course and the more recent Glashedy course, which threads its way through the centre and around the outside of the Old Course. Thanks to the extended fringe at the back of the par-4, 13th green, the Old Course bags the title of 'Most Northerly Golf Course in Ireland', but not by more than a few yards, from Glashedy's 12th hole fairway.

Golf in Ireland has seen a boom with the growth of the 'Celtic Tiger' economy in the 1990s and the rise of golf tourism, so it would be easy to think that the Ballyliffin Club enjoyed a nice comfortable existence as a local club, before cashing in with a second 18 holes when membership and visitors began to ramp up. Far from it.

As the club history reveals, its development was painstakingly slow, a similar story to many of the Irish clubs that have existed and struggled along thanks to the dedication of local golfers. This is no Old Head of Kinsale.

Founded in 1947, land at Pollan Green was leased from local farmers for a nine-hole golf course, while the Strand Hotel served as the clubhouse. One of the major events of 1948 was the purchase of a £10 Atco motor mower. Sadly this proved unreliable, so before their round of golf, members brought along their own lawnmowers to cut the

greens and tees. They also needed to check the wire that enclosed the greens, a method still in place in Barra and other parts of the Western Isles of Scotland which play across common grazing land and are clubs dependent on community help. Course maintenance first — the game of golf second.

When the lease on the commonly owned land ran out in 1969, a tricky negotiation involved buying out the farmers who held grazing rights across the course. It was by no means a straightforward matter. After a long process of tactful negotiation, the club offered each farmer £500 a share and the 400 acres of land that swept along the edge of Pollan Strand was theirs. With a view to a bright future they employed a full-time greenkeeper.

The 'new' Old Course was largely put together by the grand old man of Irish golf, Eddie Hackett (Waterville) and opened in 1973. Despite the expanded course and the quality of the golf holes, Ballyliffin was dogged by financial problems through the 1970s, and they were only turned around in 1987 when a newly built clubhouse started to attract golf societies scared away by the old prefabricated building.

In the early 1990s the club wanted to build on the success and consultants brought in believed they could do so much more with their 400 acres. When the club had expanded from nine to 18 holes money was tight and so Eddie

Hackett's course rambled around the land. With some of the best links turf in Ireland to play with they suggested a new championship-standard course that could fit in between the Old Course holes with not much bother. The Glashedy course made its debut in 1995 to great acclaim and Ballyliffin took its place as one of the great golfing destinations of Ireland. It is a far more engaging story than a multi-millionaire or golf investment fund buying a piece of treasured coastal land, building a course and hiring a PR firm to big it up.

The Old is still a classic links, with fairways that buck and roll, pitch and wander through wild timeless dunes, and where perfectly straight fairway drives can be rewarded with awkward bounces and an unseen scurry into the rough.

The irrepressible Pat Ruddy, Irish golf architect, author and raconteur helped bring the Glashedy course to life, and part of his work was nudging the Old Course in places, so that the new 18 holes of Glashedy fitted as seamlessly as the topography allowed.

The Glashedy course is a true championship test which can be 7,200 yards from the back tees. It has nine par-4s in excess of 400 yards to vouch for that, though the fairways are flatter and bounces fairer. Golfers come to Glashedy for the challenge and the Old Course for the charm. In 2018 the championship course hosted the Irish Open. Not bad for a club that 60 years earlier was mowing its own greens.

ONE OF THE MOST REMARKABLE GOLF COURSES IN THE WORLD, IT IS TURNBERRY, PEBBLE BEACH AND SHEEP RANCH ROLLED INTO ONE

OLD HEAD GOLF LINKS

KINSALE, COUNTY CORK, IRELAND

The Old Head of Kinsale is the most dramatic of landscapes on which to plant a golf course. Almost any coastal course that commands the heights will benefit from impressive views, but at some point they have to turn inland. The Old Head Links (where they got the idea of 'links' from is hard to fathom, it's at Tralee, Lahinch and Ballybunion that you get sand between your toes) is like playing around a small rocky island attached to the mainland by a thin peninsula.

The idea to develop a golf course at Old Head was conceived by brothers John and Patrick O'Connor in the late 1980s when they acquired the rugged County Cork coastal promontory. It was a site rich in history, with ruined castle towers and a long-maintained lighthouse, plus an abundance of wildlife, so there were many stakeholders to appease before planning permission was given and the club could open in 1997.

It was an immediate success, a supercharged Turnberry that could take its place in any golf tour alongside the storied courses of Ireland's wild Atlantic coast. It was designed as a walking course to help it blend in with the natural landscape — although the insurance premium on golf buggies might have been as difficult as the 12th hole. This is 'Courcean Stage', a 560-yard, par-5 and the only hole to venture up the peninsula. It demands an accurate drive to a tight fairway, all the while resisting the extra gravity of the cliff on the left and mindful of the prevailing wind. Given its exposed and lofty elevation it can get 'fierce windy' on the diamond-shaped headland.

Trusted course reviewer David Jones (AKA UK Golf Guy) put into words what many feel when they're playing the vertiginous course: 'The cliff edges don't have any walls running alongside and even though you know it is very unlikely you will find yourself tumbling down a cliffside, it does play tricks with the mind.'

But it's an exhilarating kind of fear, one that sharpens the senses and makes good shots seem even better. The course measures 7,100 yards from the back tees, 5,413 yards from the front, and there are often six tees for every hole. Nine of the holes play along the 300-foot-high cliff tops, so it might not be an idea to bring your favourite ball to the course. The par-4, 4th, 'Razor's Edge', with a green installed below the lighthouse is perhaps the most photographed of them all.

In total there are five par-5s, five par-3s and eight par-4s making up one of the most spectacular rounds of golf you could play in the Emerald Isle. Back in the clubhouse, there is a *Lusitania*-themed bar to reflect on your round and plan a return. The famous transatlantic liner RMS *Lusitania* was sunk by German torpedoes on its way from New York to Liverpool in 1915 just eleven miles out from the Head of Kinsale. For those wishing to know more, there is a small museum at the Old Head Signal Tower, right outside the club's entrance. The price of admission is a lot less than the round of golf.

ORIGINALLY ONE OF THE GREAT VICTORIAN GOLF HOTELS, ROSAPENNA HAS BEEN REBORN AS A MODERN MULTI-COURSE RESORT

ROSAPENNA RESORT

ROSAPENNA, DONEGAL, IRELAND

The parallels of the Rosapenna golf courses and those of nearby Ballyliffin are many. Both are located on the north-western shore of Donegal, both were off the beaten golf track until their 'old' courses were eclipsed by the addition of fantastic modern courses which have created a resurgence of interest in the originals.

But the genesis of today's Rosapenna Resort could not be more different from Ballyliffin. It was conceived in the nineteenth century by Robert Clements, the 4th Earl of Leitrim, as a health resort offering a private 3-mile sandy beach for walks along Sheephaven Bay. There was lawn tennis and croquet, boating, bathing, saltwater angling and, if one fancied, freshwater fishing could be arranged on rivers on the Earl's estate. Old Tom Morris was employed to create a nine-hole golf course on this perfect links land.

The centrepiece was the Rosapenna Hotel, built from Norwegian pine, combining features of Norwegian inns and Swiss chalets. Sadly the earl died of blood poisoning in 1892 after his return from Scandinavia to buy the timber. Nevertheless the hotel was opened in 1893 and marketed as 'Norway in Ireland'.

Like so many old courses, it has been reworked by a number of famous names in its lifetime. Harry Vardon was invited along in 1906 to expand it from nine holes, and subsequently James Braid and Harry Colt made improvements. This would have been the layout played by Hollywood greats Errol Flynn and John Wayne who visited Rosapenna before the hotel's demise. Fire ripped through

the building in 1962 and it was not rebuilt. Instead, the adjacent Sheephaven House was transformed into a small 12-bedroomed hotel with bar and clubhouse (not unlike The Strand at Ballyliffin). The property was bought in 1981 by local business people Frank and Hilary Casey, who set about creating what would become, over the next four decades, the Rosapenna Resort.

Twenty years on, celebrated Irish golf architect Pat Ruddy (The European) was brought in to create another, more adventurous course on the land overlooking Sheephaven Bay. Following on from his work at Ballyliffin, Ruddy jostled the old course around to fit in the new 18 holes which would be Sandy Hills. On the front nine, players

are often required to carry to the green. However, on the back nine, there are more opportunities to run the ball onto the putting surface.

Even though they had 36 fine holes the ambitious Casey family, whose sons became part of the business, saw the possibility of expanding further. Along the Bay, a mile or so to the south of Rosapenna, lay another piece of land which was to become St Patrick's Links.

The site had been big enough for the building of two golf courses in the past — and would have given visitors to this magnificent corner of Donegal 72 holes spread around the bay. But it's a cautionary tale for those who develop golf courses. Both were bought up by a company

which drafted in Jack Nicklaus's expertise to create more modern tracks, on a grander scale, and with the cachet of the Golden Bear logo. Having started the groundwork, the company behind the scheme filed for bankruptcy and the land was left to nature.

The Caseys stepped in. Following stiff environmental planning laws introduced in the mid 1990s, land with planning permission for golf courses in Ireland was extremely difficult to come by. Ballyliffin had rushed through the Glashedy course to dodge them. The Rosapenna Resort was perfectly placed to take advantage of this land set up for golf, and got on the phone to Tom Doak. Instead of two courses, they let his creative team have the whole plot for

18 holes and Doak didn't disappoint. St Patrick's Links when it opened in 2021 received rapturous reviews across the golfing press. It is a course to be enjoyed, not fought — and as the greens mature, it can only get better.

"People come to play Royal County Down, Royal Portrush, Castlerock and Portstewart and then Ballyliffin, Rosapenna, Murvagh, Enniscrone and Rosses Point before heading back to Dublin," said Frank Casey Jnr. "We are only three-and-a-half hours from the airport." It's certainly a lot easier than in the 1890s when tourists needed to take a steamboat from Glasgow to get to Rosapenna.

Opposite top Looking back towards
Newcastle and the distinctive
rooftops of the Slieve Donard Hotel.

Opposite bottom A dogleg that cannot
be cut, the majestic 9th hole on the
Annesley Links course.

Above An aerial view of the course
set up for the R&A Women's Amateur
Championship in 2019.

ROYAL COUNTY DOWN

NEWCASTLE, COUNTY DOWN, NORTHERN IRELAND

Royal County Down Golf Club is in a beautiful spot, where the Mountains of Mourne sweep down to the sea. Set on the natural links land bordering Dundrum Bay it is overlooked by the distinctive slopes of Slieve Donard which rises to 2,789 feet (850m).

Prolific golf guide writer of the early twentieth century Bernard Darwin (grandson of Charles) described the joy of sweeping back his hotel curtains and seeing the mountain, knowing that he had a morning playing a course of... 'big and glorious carries, nestling greens, entertainingly blind shots, local knowledge and beautiful turf — the kind of golf that people play in their most ecstatic dreams.' Most golfers would not describe a succession of blind shots as entertaining, but Darwin might have been playing with a forecaddie.

Nine holes had been laid out for play in 1889 and later that year Old Tom Morris extended that number to 18 for the princely sum of four guineas. Harry Vardon — who seems to have spent his life modifying Old Tom's work — updated the course in 1908, after which King Edward VII gave his royal patronage.

In Darwin's short summation of the course there is a lot of truth. Measuring nearly 7,200 yards from the back tees, Royal County Down is brutishly difficult, with many blind shots for which local knowledge (or a website flyover) is needed. The 4th hole, at the far end of the course, faces back towards the town and mountains and is a picturesque but scary 228-yard, par-3. It requires a tee shot to carry gorse bushes, avoid ten bunkers, some of them 'bearded' with coarse grass at the top, and stop short of more gorse bushes at the back.

In between the holes of the Championship course has been threaded the Annesley links, a short and tight 4,548-yard course with no par-5s and a par of 66. It's a modest challenge compared to the older course, which is rated as one of the world's very best. But high handicappers are likely to see a lot more of their ball on the Annesley — and the views are almost the same.

141

Left An aerial view of the two courses at Royal Portrush. In the foreground the Dunluce Championship Course and beyond, approaching the town of Portrush, the Valley Links.

GOLFERS RARELY GET DISTRACTED BY A SEA VIEW ON THIS MOST TESTING OF OPEN CHAMPIONSHIP COURSES

ROYAL PORTRUSH

PORTRUSH, COUNTY ANTRIM, NORTHERN IRELAND

Situated on the North Antrim coast of Northern Ireland, Royal Portrush has been hosting golf since the formation of the County Club in 1888 and thanks to patronage by the playboy Prince of Wales, assumed its current name in 1895. However, don't assume that the name means it's a stuffy throwback to older days — visitors are welcomed.

From the links, golfers can look towards Malin Head in Donegal or north to the Isle of Islay in the Scottish Hebrides. There are two courses. The main track is the Dunluce Championship Course to the east of the site at Portrush. It takes its name from the romantic ruin, the 13th century Dunluce Castle which overlooks the links beyond the White Rocks. This is the course that hosted the Open Championship in 1951 and returned to the rota in 2019 with Shane Lowry's popular win, six strokes clear of Tommy Fleetwood.

The second course is the Valley Links, shorter and gentler than Dunluce and closer both to Portrush town and the sea. That doesn't mean that golfers playing the shorter course will be looking out to sea. With its high dunes at the shore edge, the name of the course signifies that fairways run along the dune valleys formed over thousands of years by time and tide.

Ironically, though mostly routed inland from the coast, the Dunluce course presents the best sea views especially from the 5th green and the 6th tee which teeter at the edge of the cliff. Fairways are reputed to give fair, straightforward

bounces off its ancient turf, yet the Dunluce still has some very intimidating holes. The par-4, 4th hole, 'Fred Daly's', is more than 480 yards from the back tees, with out of bounds right, craftily positioned fairway bunkers and dense rough on the left. The 5th hole, 'White Rocks', at 380 yards is the only par-4 under 400 yards but overhit an approach shot and the ball will disappear over the cliff edge to be welcomed by the North Atlantic.

The 16th hole, named 'Calamity Corner' (perhaps the precursor to 'Amen Corner'), is a fearsome 236-yard, uphill par-3. It is played to a green over a deep rough hollow, though as a concession to those who don't want to go for the pin, there is a lengthy apron to the left. 'Calamity'

is followed by the 17th, 'Purgatory', which may be what American golfer J.B. Holmes went through in the 2019 Open. Heading into the final round at -10 and in a clear third place behind Lowry and Fleetwood he shot a 16-over-par 87 and finished at +6.

For *Game of Thrones* fans, those who like to combine golf with sightseeing Royal Portrush is close to the harbour of Ballintoy, which featured the coastal pier where Theon Greyjoy arrives back in the Iron Islands. Round the corner is the Carrick-a-Rede rope bridge which Balon Greyjoy was thrown off by his brother and not so far inland is the famous Dark Hedges, the road to Kings Landing.

GOLFERS LOVE THE REMOTE CHARM
OF THIS LINKS COURSE BLESSED WITH
ITS RUGGED DUNES AND WATER ON
THREE SIDES

Opposite top An aerial view of the
par-4, 16th hole curling around the
entrance to the Rinny River estuary.

Opposite bottom Looking down on
the 15th fairway and green, with the
par-3, 4th green to the right.

Above The par-4, 2nd hole at
Waterville with great views across to
the Aghatubrid mountain.

WATERVILLE GOLF CLUB
WATERVILLE, COUNTY KERRY, IRELAND

Although a keen golfer and member of the Riviera Country
Club, Charlie Chaplin would have been unable to play a round
of golf in Waterville on one of his many family holidays. For
a decade starting in 1959, Chaplin rook rooms at the Butler
Arms Hotel in Waterville. He had no links to Ireland, made
no films there, but just loved the peace and quiet of the
small village overlooked by Macgillycuddy's Reeks, Ireland's
highest mountain range.

It is this serene beauty that can be so beguiling on the
right afternoon to play golf. There had been a nine-hole
course laid out on the promontory overlooking Ballinskelligs
Bay since 1889, but the club closed in the 1950s and that
looked like that. Enter Jack Mulcahy an American with
Irish roots who bought the club in the late 1960s and
commissioned 1948 Masters champion Claude Harmon,
together with prolific Irish architect Eddie Hackett, to design
an 18-hole course in its place.

The new course was opened in 1973 and like a good
Irish whiskey has matured with age. Very much like the Old
Course at Ballybunion, the front nine stays on the gentle

flat, with holes abutting the River Rinny estuary, before
tackling the higher dunes of the back nine which border
the sea. Standout holes include the 366-yard, par-4, 16th,
once called 'Round the Bend' because the fairway doglegs
around the outside edge of the spit separating estuary from
Atlantic. Then it's time to climb up to a raised tee and admire
a grand view across the course from the 17th, 'Mulcahy's
Peak'. It's an 194-yard slightly downhill lob onto the green,
before a 585-yard, par-5 takes players home along the edge
of the ocean.

Tiger Woods and friend Mark O'Meara thought it
the perfect place to prepare together for the Open
Championship. "There are few courses that can compare
to the remote beauty of Waterville," said O'Meara. And the
much-missed Payne Stewart was thinking along the same
lines as Chaplin: "Waterville gives me peace. It's one of the
few places where I can totally relax." Stewart was due to
be Honorary Captain of Waterville in 2000, before his plane
went down in South Dakota. Pinehurst is not the only golf
course with a Payne Stewart statue.

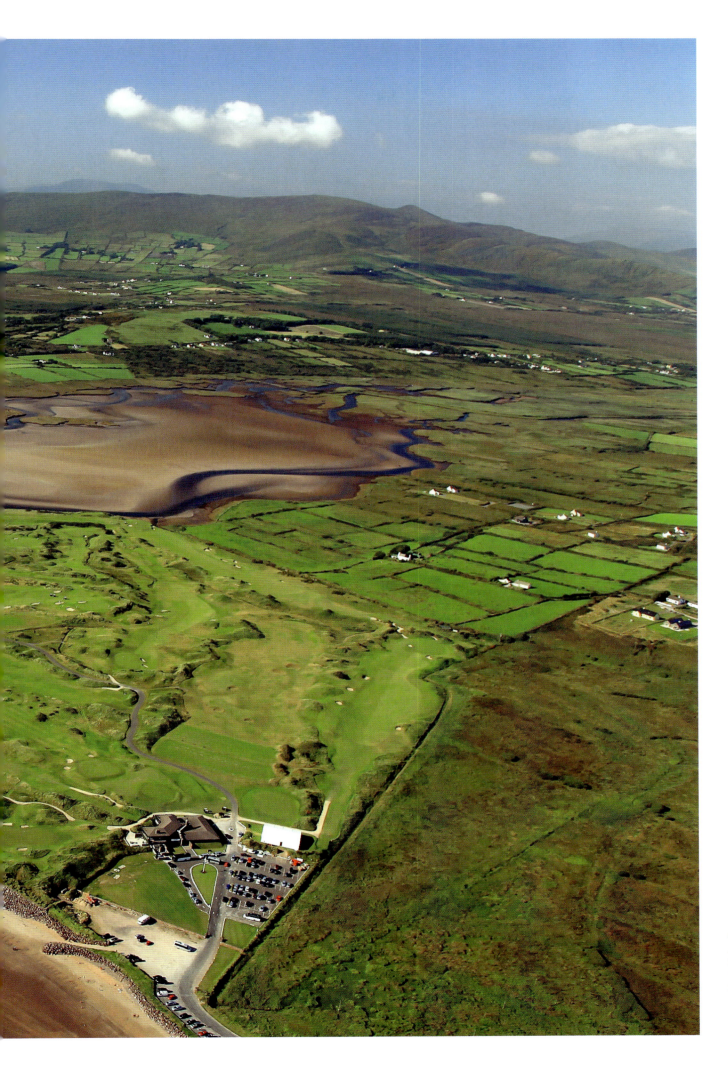

Left The glorious expanse of Waterville Golf Club occupying the land between the River Rinny estuary and the North Atlantic.

LOFOTEN LINKS

BRAUTARHOLT GOLF CLUB

GOLF D' ÉTRETAT

REAL GOLF
DE PEDREÑA

MARCO SIMONE
GOLF CLUB

REAL CLUB
VALDERRAMA

EUROPE

THERE IS A STARK BEAUTY ABOUT ICELAND'S MANY GOLF COURSES, OF WHICH BRAUTARHOLT IS THE GREATEST EXAMPLE

Opposite top Looking back down the par-5, opening hole. Beyond the edge of the green it's a sheer drop.

Opposite bottom Iceland is the land of ice and fire ... and water, with many freshwater lagoons to dodge on the 7th hole.

Above The par-5, 9th green set in the rawest of landscapes.

BRAUTARHOLT GOLF CLUB
BRAUTARHOLT, REYKYAVIK, ICELAND

The golf club at Brautarholt may only be a 30-minute drive from Iceland's capital Reykyavik, but get out on the course and it is like playing golf in a wilderness. Stretching around rugged bays the 12-hole track has all the primal volcanic surroundings of Hawaii, combined with the climate and seabird population of Scotland.

Brautarholt is the Land of Ice and Fire's most stunning example of which there are many contenders. A course at Hornafjörður is played against the backdrop of the Vatnajökull glacier, while the Geysir course is surrounded by old lava flows and the sulphurous whiff of geothermal activity nearby.

There is a long-established golf course on the southwestern island of Vestmannaeyjar which golfers liken to playing a round on a *Lord of the Rings* set.

Golf is the people's game in Iceland, with the greatest percentage of players per head of population than any country in the world. They have the land and the rain for it and there are 11 courses in the Greater Reykyavik area. But that interest has to be crammed into a very short space of time. Brautarholt is only playable from May to September. The offset is that with constant daylight through mid-summer, players can tee off at 3 a.m. in the morning.

Brautarholt is the work of golf architect Edwin Roald, the Icelandic Tom Doak, and is the pioneer (or should that be the revivalist) of 12-hole courses. It started off as a nine- in 2011 and then Roald added three more holes in 2017. It's a course rich in water hazards, both saltwater and freshwater, with some greens of epic scale. It's a course that's fully engaging to play, which begs a photo at almost every hole.

GOLF D'ÉTRETAT

ÉTRETAT, NORMANDY, FRANCE

The chalk belt that forms the white cliffs of Dover, runs under the channel and emerges in Normandy at Dieppe and Étretat. The small fishing village was thick with *Anglais* at the turn of the century, and, as at Dinard (1887), they felt a pressing need to build a golf club. Thus in 1908 Bernard Forbes, 8th Earl of Granard, found himself president of one of the earliest clubs in France along with a cast of characters straight out of a P.G. Wodehouse novel.

They employed Frenchmen Julien Chantepie and Arnaud Massy to design them a course. Massy was the first non-Brit to win the Open Championship, at Royal Liverpool, in 1907. He had learned his golf playing the links of North Berwick and married a Scots girl. He was so delighted with his victory that he named his daughter Hoylake.

The course he established is little changed today, with some magnificent sea views *of* the chalk cliffs and *from*

the chalk cliffs, back down to the picturesque town below. The most photogenic of them is the par-5, 10th hole which sweeps up the hill from the town to a headland flanked by two chalk arches. The 11th is a short hole inland, and then the 12th, 13th and 14th all follow the cliff edge in an exhilarating sequence.

The green fees at Étretat are surprisingly modest for such a dramatic round of golf, and especially good value out of season, when playing on well-drained chalk should not be a handicap. With the clubhouse down in the town, there are plenty of gastronomic diversions afterwards. The biggest drawback, as in any European venue, is the constant translation of metres to yards (something scrupulously ignored in this book). Although phrases such as '*Merci de ratisser les bunkers après votre passage*' are quite easy to understand.

ONE OF THE WORLD'S MOST
NORTHERLY GOLF COURSES, IT'S
WORTH THE JOURNEY TO PLAY GOLF
IN THE LAND OF THE MIDNIGHT SUN

Opposite top One of photographer
Gary Lisbon's favourite holes, the
par-3, 2nd at Lofoten Links.

Opposite bottom The par-4, 16th
green with plenty of danger both left
and right for those who drive long.

Above Precision is needed yet again
on the 400-yard, par-4, 14th hole
skirting the rocky shoreline.

LOFOTEN LINKS

GIMSØYSAND, NORWAY

There's a little bit of Mexico off the Norwegian coast. The fabulous links course only opened on the island of Gimsøya in 2015, but it already has a celebrated hole. The green for the short par-3, 2nd hole sits on a little rocky outcrop surrounded by ocean. It's the spitting image of Jack Nicklaus's 'Tale of the Whale' island hole at Punta Mita, except in this instance nature has provided an isthmus for easy access.

The next hole is interesting too. It's a 435-yard, par-4 with a dogleg at almost right-angles to the left, which would be tempting for powerful hitters bar the fact that there is sea, beach and foreshore that bites into the fairway and any failed attempt would be down amongst the local shellfish.

It's a short course, 6,429 yards in length, with six glorious holes besides the seaside, including the 3rd and 17th greens which argue for space next to one another and

could easily become a double green. There's more water inland with a large freshwater lake to cross, or gingerly skirt, on two holes and one guarding the approach to the short par-4, 9th.

In many respects it's like golf in Iceland a thousand years later, after moss, lichen, heather and gorse have colonized the raw igneous landscape and the weather has softened the edges. Similarly, it can only be played in the summer months, when days are endless and when nights do finally arrive there's a chance of glimpsing the Northern Lights.

The landscape of the Lofoten Links is inspirational and the course is easily a match for the views. If only it weren't so difficult to get there. You don't need to be Roald Amundsen to get to this course in the Arctic Circle, but you do need at least some of his dedication. But what a course awaits you...

Left The short par-4 opening hole at Lofoten Links sets the tone for what will be a jaw-dropping round of golf.

MARCO SIMONE GOLF CLUB

GUIDONIA MONTECELIO, ITALY

Marco Simone Golf and Country Club sounds like it might be the creation of some Italian businessman in the mould of Luciano Benetton, but the course is named after the 1,000-year-old castle Marco Simone.

Located ten miles outside of Rome near the historic hill town of Tivoli, it was a course reworked with matchplay in mind, focusing on that much-loved term 'risk and reward', with wide spacing between fairways to allow for the anticipated tournament spectators. Understandably, some very distant back tees were added, especially at the 12th where the back tee is at 551 yards and the forward at 421 yards. If visitors strained their eyes from some of the higher spots, they might also catch a glimpse of St Peter's Basilica and the Eternal City in the far distance.

It was first put together by Jim Fazio in 1989 and then altered by cousin Tom Fazio II, keeping it in the family. After Marco Simone was given the nod as Ryder Cup hosts in 2015, Tom's work was very much focused on creating a course that could light up the competition, and in the land of the Molinari brothers he certainly pulled it off.

The par-3, 2nd hole gives the best views of the old fortified farmhouse that has been given the slightly grand title of castle. Not that many of the competitors in golf's greatest team contest were taking architectural notes. The 18th hole is a fitting conclusion for a grand competition, a 597-yard par-5 with water to the left of the green and significantly, two lifebelts... Because you always have to prepare for that Paul McGinley moment.

HARRY COLT'S PARKLAND BEAUTY GAZES OUT TO THE BAY OF SANTANDER — A COURSE THAT HELPED NURTURE A UNIQUE GOLFING TALENT

REAL GOLF DE PEDREÑA

PEDREÑA, CANTABRIA, SPAIN

Although Spain is often seen as a latecomer to golf, Real Golf de Pedreña is four years older than Augusta National. It was designed by the great Harry Colt on a promontory overlooking the city of Santander on Spain's northern coast, and opened in 1928. The 18 holes range through mature parkland with views down onto the ría de Cubas and its meandering estuary to the east, and on the seaward side, the Bay of Santander.

It is not too hard to guess the name of the local lad who made a name for himself on his home course of Pedreña when he captured the 1975 Spanish Under-25 Championship at just 17 years of age. Severiano Ballesteros helped transform the image of Spanish golf, a torch taken on by Olazábal, Garcia and today Jon Rahm.

The 18 holes of the 6,340-yard course where Seve learned his trade come in at a par of 70. One of the most admired holes is the par-3, 10th, a typical 'redan' hole with the green angled away, two hefty bunkers guarding the front and a rippling green that takes the contours of the hill through to the putting surface.

There has been much reconfiguring of Harry's work over the years, including the exclusion and readmission of the 10th, but the most impactful change in recent years has involved a chainsaw. To supplement the natural woodland, many trees were planted in the early years to separate out the fairways. After reaching maturity, they closed in the course and obscured some of the impressive views of sea, estuary and mountain (they also provided obstacles around which the young Seve could learn to bend shots).

To restore the course to its original Colt configuration many trees have been removed, for the same reason that Oakmont divested itself of its timber, and the result is a round of golf that both challenges and presents some inspiring views.

THE CLUB'S AMBITIOUS OWNER TRANSFORMED A REGULAR 'COSTA DEL GOLF' COURSE INTO A CHAMPIONSHIP HOSTING VENUE

REAL CLUB VALDERRAMA
SOTOGRANDE, ANDALUSIA, SPAIN

Valderrama started life with humble intentions. It was the course linked to a large housing development built around old Sotogrande, in Andalusia and known as 'Sotogrande New'. Robert Trent Jones Sr. had started the golf ball rolling by designing Real Club de Golf Sotogrande in 1964.

So he seemed the perfect choice to design this important villa sales feature in 1974. Renamed 'Las Aves' in 1981, it was then acquired by Bolivian industrialist and art collector Jaime Ortiz-Patiño who wanted to make it a premier golfing destination.

The billionaire businessman spent a small fortune reworking what was an average course — again assisted by Trent Jones — into what he believed to be 'the Augusta of Europe'. He christened his new project Valderrama.

There is no doubt it is a fantastic course, though matching Augusta is a hard ask. It became the first European mainland destination for the Ryder Cup in 1997 with the European side captained by Severiano Ballesteros, and it also hosted the Volvo Masters for a decade.

One of the most photographed holes is the par-5, 4th which launches off a high tee with a view of a far-distant green nestled amongst cork oaks. Valderrama was an early adopter of waterfalls in unlikely places and one protects the front edge of the green, giving it the name 'Las Cascada'.

The closing holes are resolutely difficult, with the par-5, 17th, 'Los Gabiones', now one of the toughest, having had an expanse of water placed in front of the green — the way Wentworth have remodelled the 18th — so that players entertain more risk if they want to make the green in two.

Since it was built, more clubs have arrived in southern Andalucia which is now home to more than 15 courses. But Valderrama is the best.

NEFYN GOLF CLUB

ROYAL WEST NORFOLK
GOLF CLUB

ROYAL ST DAVID'S GOLF CLUB

ROYAL LIVERPOOL
GOLF CLUB

ROYAL ST GEORGE'S

PENNARD GOLF CLUB

WENTWORTH
WEST COURSE

SUNNINGDALE OLD COURSE

HANKLEY COMMON
GOLF CLUB

ENGLAND AND WALES

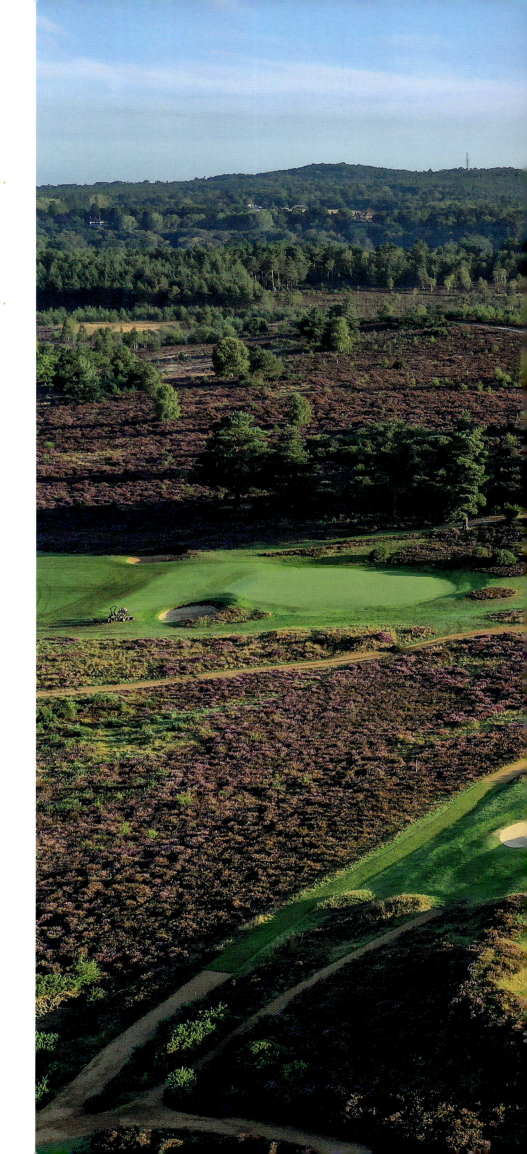

RIVALLING GLENEAGLES FOR ITS DRAMATIC HOLES PLAYED THROUGH AN OCEAN OF PURPLE HEATHER

HANKLEY COMMON GOLF CLUB

TILFORD, SURREY, ENGLAND

Hankley Common is well known to the UK's film industry. The vast expanse of heathland in Surrey, previously used for military training (including a mock-up of the Atlantic Wall which troops practised storming to prepare for D-Day) has been the backdrop for many movies including *Skyfall*, *1917*, *Black Widow* and *Napoleon*.

Golf came to Hankley in 1897 with an initial nine holes, after which James Braid added a further nine in 1922. Master improver Harry Colt applied his sure touch in 1936, and Hankley Common became a match for Surrey's more famous heathland courses, such as Walton Heath and Sunningdale.

What makes Hankley Common distinct is the sheer spaciousness of the course. The 18 holes cover 164 acres, but it is set in an estate of 850 acres rich in heathland flora and fauna — heather, birch, rowan and Scots pine. It's a site of Special Scientific Interest where some of the trees have been removed to allow greater expanses of heather and the species that thrive alongside it. Thus in August and September the course is swathed in a mass of purple accompanied by the hum of bees collecting from this rich source of nectar.

The R&A's favoured course tweakers Mackenzie & Ebert were employed by the club to add length and variety for 2023. One review described their new par-3, 2nd hole as, 'a little bit of Pine Valley in Surrey'. High praise indeed. It was also the year in which Hankley hosted the final qualifying round for the Women's Open Championship held at Walton Heath and so players would have been well-versed at the folly of straying into the heather.

FOR GOLFERS THAT VALUE A SEA
VIEW ABOVE ANYTHING ELSE –
THERE'S ONE FROM EVERY TEE

Above Llanmynech lad Ian Woosnam
ranks Nefyn among his favourite
courses and holds the club record
with a 67. A view of the par-3,3rd hole.

Opposite The peninsula holes are part
of the 'Old Nine' with the tiny village
of Porthdinllaen nestled below the
cliffs.

NEFYN GOLF CLUB

NEFYN, GWYNEDD, NORTH WALES

Clwb Golff Nefyn/Nefyn Golf Club has been described by
visitors as Wales's answer to Pebble Beach, but its sheer
elevation makes it more like Turnberry in Ayrshire, or even
Old Head of Kinsale without the lighthouse.

The voice of golf for many decades, Peter Alliss, rated
it as one of his ten favourite courses in a list that included
Sunningdale and St Andrews: 'A truly spectacular golfing
location in North West Wales which boasts a rich variety
of majestic and challenging holes on its 6,500-yard
Championship course, set against the stunning backdrop of
Snowdonia and the Irish Sea. The welcome and the sheer
beauty of the place will take your breath away.'

Situated on the north coast of the Llŷn peninsula and
perched on the sea cliffs overlooking Porthdinllaen bay, it
started life as a nine-hole course in 1907, added a further
nine in 1912, and ventured inland for a further nine holes in
1933. One of its rare distinctions is that there is a sea view
from each of its 27 tees.

The most photographed of its holes and the most
popular are on the original nine-hole Point Course with its

narrow fairways and elevated tees and greens that run along
the peninsula to the lifeboat station. Nefyn faces the same
challenges as both Pebble Beach and Old Head of Kinsale in
that greens and fairways can fall victim to storm damage,
as happened in 2013, when salt water wrecked the grass,
causing the closure of the peninsula holes for 18 months.
Luckily with another 18 holes to fall back on, members
weren't deprived of either play or sea views while the
restoration was in progress.

One other tantalizing prospect for visitors to Nefyn
is a visit to the Ty Coch Inn down in the tiny village of
Porthdinllaen nestled under the cliffs below the sixth green.
It can only be reached on foot by non-residents, visitors
must park either at the National Trust or pay a charge at the
golf club. Given his love of the course Peter Alliss was happy
to supply the voiceover for the club's hole-by-hole flyover,
recorded in 2015, and unsurprisingly mentions the 'Red
House' pub in what is a nostalgic listen: "You can go there
for a pint before you tackle the last three holes. Sometimes
you need more than a pint, you need a large one."

Right Nefyn has been described as Wales's answer to Pebble Beach. Situated on the Llŷn Peninsula in North Wales it was one of Peter Alliss's favourite courses and the club website still features hole-by-hole commentary from the voice of BBC golf.

'THE LINKS IN THE SKY' THREADS ITS WAY THROUGH A HISTORIC LANDSCAPE AND OVERLOOKS ONE OF SOUTH WALES' MOST TREASURED BEACHES

PENNARD GOLF CLUB

PENNARD, SWANSEA, WALES

Set on the Gower peninsula, a few miles out of Swansea and close to one of Dylan Thomas's seaside haunts, Pennard Golf Club was an undiscovered gem for many years. It commands a hillside overlooking the magnificent Three Cliffs Bay.

But the terrain above the limestone cliffs is not what you might expect. Further out on Gower, towards Oxwich bay and Rhossili, after 200 feet of elevation the cliffs give way to open farmland. At Pennard it's a surprise to find dunes rolling across the headland that mimic the humps and hollows of traditional sea-level links. It is why Pennard Golf Club has gained the epithet 'the links in the sky'. With the occasional cow.

Golf was played across the hillside from 1896, until in 1908 Pennard Golf Club formalized things and employed James Braid to lay out 18 holes. In 1996 Tom Doak's *The Confidential Guide To Golf Courses*, which reviewed courses from around the world, truly put Pennard on

the map. 'One of my all-time favourites, but I hesitate to recommend it for general consumption; it's awfully quirky. The site, on a promontory of undulating ground between the sea and the 'Pennard Pill' (a deep stream valley), is one of the most spectacular I've ever seen.'

Throw in a romantic ruin of a Norman castle which has been overwhelmed by the dunes that massed around its battlements, and you have a unique course. As Doak implied, it has its quirks. For the par-4, 7th, 'Castle', players must drive down a tumbling fairway between a church ruin and the old castle to a punchbowl green. There players are rewarded with a grand vista of Three Cliffs Bay beyond. There are blind shots and sloping fairways to contend with and a handful of wonderfully contoured greens. Bernard Darwin also noted the course's ability to surprise. And that doesn't include the grazing cattle that from time to time roam across the scenery.

LOCATED AT THE EDGE OF THE
DEE ESTUARY, HOYLAKE HAS BEEN
HOSTING OPEN CHAMPIONSHIPS
SINCE 1897

Opposite A view from the tee of the par-3, 11th hole, ironically named 'Alps'. It played as the 13th hole in the 2023 Open Championship.

Above The 134-yard, par-3, 15th hole 'Little Eye' which played as the 17th hole in the 2023 Open.

ROYAL LIVERPOOL GOLF CLUB
HOYLAKE, CHESHIRE, ENGLAND

Old Tom Morris didn't get all the commissions. When the Liverpool Golf Club were looking for someone to lay out their course in 1869 they opted for younger brother George Morris, who planned out the first nine holes along with Robert Chambers (a talented Edinburgh amateur golfer who had placed 10th in the 1861 Open and was part of the publishing firm responsible for *Chambers English Dictionary*).

The inevitable Harry Colt followed on and redesigned what had become 18 holes in the early twentieth century. As golf balls flew further and clubs changed from hickory to steel to graphite, so the course has been lengthened, but the essential character of the course is as traditional as the venerable clubhouse.

Located at the tip of the Wirral peninsula between the towns of Hoylake and West Kirby it is often referred to as 'Hoylake' instead of Royal Liverpool because it is 12 miles from Liverpool, across the county border and much simpler, especially after the club received royal patronage in 1871.

Holes 11–14 delight the eye by playing along the coastline with the Dee estuary beyond and the farm land of North Wales on the far shore. The sea's edge is revisited one final time for the short par-3, 17th hole, 'Little Eye'. This is a recent introduction grafted onto the course at the exact corner of the Wirral. It's a hole loaded with potential grief for an inaccurate tee-shot, elevated above its surrounds and encircled by sand which will welcome most

balls that fail to come to rest on the putting surface.

For the professional golfers, there are two 600+ yard par-5s which can cause bother when the wind is strong and against, but on balmy summer days when the course is bone dry, the ball will just run and run. This is what Tiger Woods found in 2006 when he used his driver just once. Contrast that with Brian Harman's rain-lashed experience in 2023. Harman's revelation that he liked to field dress deer that he shot earned him the title 'Butcher of Hoylake' after he took the rest of the field apart.

Brian was in good company — fellow Open champions at Hoylake include Walter Hagen, J.H. Taylor, Rory McIlroy and Bobby Jones who won the title as part of his grand slam of 1930. Many of their winning scorecards are enshrined behind the memorabilia-rich club bar.

Opposite top **The 16th hole green with the Royal Liverpool clubhouse beyond. It served as the 18th hole in the 2023 Open.**

Opposite bottom **More borrows than a pawnbroker's shop — the evening sunlight reveals just how hard it is to read the 7th green.**

Above **An aerial view of the new par-3 hole, 'Little Eye' with the broad expanse of the Dee estuary beyond.**

A CHALLENGING WELSH LINKS COURSE OVERLOOKED BY THE MAGNIFICENT HARLECH CASTLE, WITH VIEWS TO MOUNT ERYRI

ROYAL ST DAVID'S GOLF CLUB

HARLECH, GWYNEDD, WALES

St David's is the smallest city in Wales, but the golf course celebrating the nation's patron saint is to be found 125 miles to the north, at the foot of Harlech Castle. It's a tremendous location, with the imposing castle surveying the land below. Indeed it is such an impregnable position that the Lancastrians withstood a seven-year siege there during the Wars of the Roses.

Both Yorkists and Lancastrians are today welcome at the club which sits on the coastal plain below the castle. Dating to 1894 and with royal patronage from 1909, it's one of the oldest clubs in Wales. It's a Jekyll and Hyde course, the first 12 holes are played over relatively flat dune hinterland, with a splash of forestry behind the 9th green. It's only when the players get to the 10th green that the great barrier of dunes is approached and the course becomes more undulating in the old tradition. Unlike the dunes of Ireland's west coast, they are tightly packed in serried ranks allowing no holes in between.

The closest golfers get to the sea is the 15th green and the 16th tee, before players drive off back inland. Throughout the round there are fabulous views across Tremadog Bay to the Llŷn peninsula, and in the distance the towering shape of Mount Eryri/Snowdon. As with Royal St George's it's now an SSSI, a Site of Special Scientific Interest, and so golfers straying into the rough duneland ecology might encounter a three-coloured dune pansy, a pyramidal orchid or even the scarce bee orchid. And wherever you are on the course, you come under the castle's unremitting gaze.

THE OPEN'S MOST POPULAR ENGLISH VENUE WAS DREAMED UP BY A SCOTSMAN TO RIVAL ST ANDREWS

ROYAL ST GEORGE'S

SANDWICH, KENT, ENGLAND

When the Open Championship finally came south of the border, it was to Royal St George's in 1894. Sandwich Bay, the area on the Kent coast northwest of Dover, was rich in championship-level links courses, with Prince's to the north, St George's in the centre and Royal Cinque Ports to the south — three old courses barely separated by a hearty whack with a baffing spoon.

The club was founded in 1887 by Edinburgh surgeon Laidlaw Purves who searched out the closest terrain to the courses he had played in Fife and East Lothian. He found wild duneland in abundance on the East Kent coast and set about laying out a course which would rival St Andrews. Saint Andrew is the patron saint of Scotland, so its counterpart was naturally the patron saint of England, Saint George.

Purves saw his great dream realized four times before his death in 1917 and would be glad to know that he created the most regularly used course for the Open in England, which held the event 15 times to 2021. This includes a stretch of 32 years without hosting an Open between 1949 and 1981.

The 1949 Open proved to be a missed chance for Irish professional Harry Bradshaw whose ball landed in the bottom of a broken beer bottle in the rough. In one of the most bizarre incidents in the history of the Open, and with no referee to consult, Bradshaw played it where it lay, shattering the glass and giving him a six for the hole.

Opposite top The only flat surface in view is the 13th green and the Prince's clubhouse car park. The 13th hole marks the northerly extent of St George's. Beyond is Prince's, an equally challenging championship course.

Opposite Bottom It's at the par-5, 7th hole that players get a real whiff of the sea from Sandwich Bay.

Above A view looking north over the sweep of the course with the 6th green below.

Left The traditional, thatched starter's hut — but with the flagtsick across the bench signifying course closed.

He finished his second round with a dispiriting 77, but still managed to equal the winning score of Bobby Locke in his final round. The 36-hole playoff was a different story.

After rebuilding three of the early holes, St George's was re-admitted to the Open rota. It is said to have the 'deepest bunker' in major championship golf, on the par-4, 4th, though this writer can attest that it should probably be billed as the 'tallest'. Author Ian Fleming used the Royal St George's course under the name 'Royal St. Marks' in his 1959 novel *Goldfinger* and it is this bunker that makes an appearance. However it is a bunker on the par-3, 17th hole that is the most notorious. At the 2003 Open, Thomas Bjørn took three shots to get out and his chance of victory slipped away.

Like many of the Open Championship courses, it is possible to play St George's as a visitor, providing players can turn up with a handicap certificate of around 18 or better. It is one of the older breed of links courses with blind shots and uneven fairways that can send straight drives scurrying towards a first cut of rough intent on hiding balls. So the insistence on a certificate is as much to preserve golfers' own peace of mind as well as to keep play moving.

It will always remain close to the heart of the 19-year-old blond lad from Ohio who won the club's Challenge Cup (established in 1888) on his first visit in 1959. Later that year he won the first of his two U.S. Amateur titles, before becoming the most successful player in the history of golf.

Opposite Buttressed by railway sleepers, the green on the par-3, 4th hole with some quintessential English seaside chalets beyond.

Above The par-4, 9th green lies a short hop across a saltmarsh spur. This is Victorian golf at its finest, played through the landscape of Dickens' *Great Expectations.*

ROYAL WEST NORFOLK GOLF CLUB
BRANCASTER, NORFOLK, ENGLAND

The Royal West Norfolk Golf Club has a lot in common with Burgh Island in Devon. Both are inaccessible at high tide. Whereas most clubs concentrate on tee times, at the course squeezed between the North Sea and the salt marshes, golfers need to pay attention to the tide times. Visitors are advised not to attempt to drive through the incoming water on Beach Road.

From the moment players step inside the Victorian clubhouse, they can appreciate the feel of an old, established links course that has hardly changed since men went out in plus-twos and wielded mashie niblicks. It was founded in 1892 on the most northerly stretch of Norfolk coast near Brancaster, a place known for its Brancaster mussels.

It's a traditional out-and-back links with nine greens abutting the sea stretching out to the 9th hole at the very easterly tip of the course, where the sea curls round into a wide creek. The 9th demands a drive over a smaller creek onto an island of fairway, to pitch over another creeklet

closer to the green. It's full of illogical old school quirks that you would never find on a modern golf course and you would never want the club to change. It starts with a drive over the edge of the 18th green.

Railway sleepers are everywhere, propping up bunkers, green edges and embankments which only add to the old world charm. Talking about the Royal Norfolk in his 1910 guide Bernard Darwin wrote that the new Haskell golf ball 'has noticeably reduced its terrors', and noted that even so, it was still a real drivers' course. These days, the yardage of 6,400 and variable compression golf balls has reduced the need to wield Callaway's latest version of the brassie. None of the par-5s are longer than 500 yards and the back nine has five par-4s under 400 yards.

Surrounded by creek, marshland and seashore, it's a place to play golf in glorious isolation. And if golfers get their tide tables wrong, that isolation can last a little longer than expected.

Opposite top A view from the tee on the par-3, 8th hole on The Old Course.

Opposite bottom A typical Sunningdale view, looking down the 5th fairway from the tee.

Above The approach to the par-4, 18th hole, complete with heather-fringed bunker and commanding oak tree overlooking the green.

SUNNINGDALE, THE OLD COURSE

SUNNINGDALE, BERKSHIRE, ENGLAND

Is Sunningdale England's Augusta — or is it England's Pine Valley with a little less sand? It is certainly one of the best maintained of the older inland courses, having settled on a spot on Sunningdale Heath in 1899. The original course was laid out by the great Willie Park Junior and after the outlay of £3,000, opened in 1901. It became the Old Course when Harry Colt — Sunningdale's first secretary and club captain — laid out the New Course in 1923.

He had already tinkered with Park's original and would go on to be consulted (along with many others) on George Crump's epic creation, Pine Valley.

Bobby Jones struck an immediate bond with Sunningdale when he came to qualify for the Open Championship in 1926. He scored a 66 and a 68 over the two rounds — the 66 consisting of 33 shots strokes and 33 putts, keeping a five off his card. Jones said afterwards: "I wish I could take this course home with me." What he *did* take home with him was a new driver made by the club pro Jack White. Jack had been the original professional at the club in 1901 and named the driver 'Jeanie Deans' after the

virtuous heroine of a Sir Walter Scott novel. Jones used it throughout his career, Jeanie accompanying him to 10 major championship victories.

Both the club and the course have old school charm — located on the belt of sandy heathland that runs through Surrey and Berkshire, home to the much-admired Berkshire and Swinley Forest courses, it possesses bunkers with heather-trimmed edges waiting to deflect any shot not perfectly flighted. Many traditional English cricket greens have large oaks that remain part of the playing area and the old oak at the back of the 18th green, the club's emblem, is a reminder of grounds like Southborough and Ickwell Green.

One unusual facet of the club is that members can bring their dogs along for a round of golf providing they are on a leash, under control at all times and are used to the sights, sounds and smells of a golf course — i.e. they don't go and retrieve a ball that has been smashed to within two feet of the pin, dragging a trolley with them. The fact that Sunningdale boasts a halfway house famed for its sausage sandwiches is surely a great incentive for any dog to keep in line.

HOME TO THE BMW CHAMPIONSHIP,
ERNIE ELS HAS ADDED WATER
TO HARRY COLT'S TRADITIONAL
HEATHLAND COURSE

WENTWORTH WEST COURSE

WENTWORTH, SURREY, ENGLAND

Wentworth is a club that's well known, but not necessarily over-played. The West Course was seared into the consciousness of the British public by its annual appearance as host of the World Match Play Championship from 1964 to 2007, in days when only the Open and highlights from Augusta would be shown on the BBC. Thus the last three clutch holes became immediately indentifiable to a generation that watched the likes of Arnold Palmer, Jack Nicklaus, Gary Player, Hale Irwin, Greg Norman, Seve Ballesteros, Sandy Lyle, Ian Woosnam and Nick Faldo lift the trophy.

Harry Colt designed both the East and West Course in the mid-1920s as part of a new concept in home building — the golf estate. Nearby in Surrey, the builder W.G. Tarrant had applied this idea in St George's Hill, Weybridge — a development of houses based on a minimum one-acre plot with a golf course at its heart. In 1922, Tarrant acquired the development rights for the estate based around the old Wentworth House. Thus, golfing for the privileged began.

Ernie Els, the club's professional-at-large (and seven times winner of the Matchplay title) was asked to make changes around the course in 2005, in particular to toughen up the final three holes. Ernie added length, repositioned bunkers, re-laid greens with more contours and added a number of water hazards close to greens. But it was his changes to the already-challenging 18th hole that divided opinion. It gained a half-encircling pond to prevent any good old-fashioned bump and runs to the green. Many thought he had disfigured the course — others applauded the update.

Despite the controversy and further calls to change the 18th, the West Course continues to host the lucrative BMW PGA Championship — very convenient to the PGA European Tour which is based at Wentworth. The club itself has changed hands several times, but is noww in the hands of new owners, who have made it even more exclusive. These days members must pay a very high price for dumping their Titleist Pro V1s into some faux pondage.

QUIVIRA

REST OF THE WORLD

HAESLEY NINE BRIDGES

ANVAYA COVE

EMIRATES GOLF CLUB

LAGUNA LĂNG CÔ

LEGEND GOLF AND SAFARI RESORT

ARABELLA COUNTRY ESTATE

A COURSE WITH TWO DIFFERENT CHARACTERS ALONG WITH SUMPTUOUS VIEWS OF THE BATAAN MOUNTAINS AND THE SOUTH CHINA SEA

Opposite top **The 11th hole takes players to the coast on the 'Seaside' nine.**

Opposite bottom **Shades of Amen Corner from Augusta National at Anvaya's testy final hole.**

Above **The idyllic location of the dogleg 12th, with its green perfectly placed for some quick beachcombing. It's probably too late in the round for a halfway stop.**

ANVAYA COVE

BARANGAY MABAYO, BATAAN, PHILIPPINES

There are many ratings handed out to golf courses around the world, but *Golf Digest* is a judge that can be relied on for telling it without fear or favour. One of their lists aggregates the best golf courses in a country and Anvaya Cove comes top for the Philippines.

Situated on the west coast of the Bataan peninsula it's a resort development with two distinct sets of nine holes — the front nine, 'Mountain', sets off inland from a variety of tees, all marked with miniature turtles. The second nine ventures out towards the sea and could have been named something grandiose like 'Ocean', but instead the owners chose 'Seaside', a far more charming name with John Betjeman overtones (the golfing Poet Laureate who wrote *Seaside Golf*).

The second nine shrugs off the resort lodges as it winds down to the South China Sea delivering great views of the Bataan mountain range. It also serves up some beautiful and challenging holes — no surprise that it was designed by Kevin Ramsey of the Californian firm Golfplan, who were behind the Haesley Nine Bridges course in South Korea.

It's at the 10th hole that Anvaya begins its march to the sea, with a 556-yard, par-5 linking hole, followed by a short downhill par-4 to an 11th green that looks very driveable, and once there, affords great views of the nearby coves and sandy beaches. At the next hole, the green is tucked round the corner by the beach, beyond a sizeable gulley that an over-ambitious drive might just tumble into. The resort has missed a trick here, this is the perfect location for a beachside stop.

Inevitably it's a trek uphill to the next, a short par-3 to a narrowing green with dense rough all around, but another great view. This is the furthest the course takes players, the tip of a peninsula — it's time to turn round and head uphill through a range of carefully thought-out holes before reaching the 18th, which has a Rae's Creek-like watercourse in front and MacKenzie-like bunkers beyond. A classic end for the Philippines' No.1.

Above Viewed from the tee of the 200-yard, par-3, 7th hole, Arabella looks like it could be a wilderness course, such is the skill of the estate developers.

Opposite top The simply beautiful par-5, 8th hole that sweeps downhill to a lakeside green.

Opposite bottom The 17th hole is a par-3 of almost 200 yards, a lakeside prelude to a striking lakeside finish.

BORDERING THE ENORMOUS BOT RIVER LAGOON, ARABELLA PRESENTS MANY REMARKABLE VISTAS AND SOME CLASSIC CLOSING HOLES

ARABELLA COUNTRY ESTATE
KLEINMOND, WESTERN CAPE, SOUTH AFRICA

For those who like to combine whale watching with golf, the Arabella Country Estate in South Africa's Western Cape is perfect. It's located close to the coastal town of Hermanus, famous for its whale watching tours around Hermanus Bay, where southern right whales often swim close to the shore.

The golf course was laid out by prolific South African course architect Peter Matkovich, the man responsible for designing many South African courses through the 1990s, occasionally venturing into nearby Zimbabwe, Swaziland and further afield to Mauritius.

When he was brought in to design the course, he found a large site of stony farmland next to the enormous Bot River Lagoon, the largest natural tidal lagoon in Southern Africa. The far side of the lagoon, which is separated from the sea by a 100-metre wide sand dune at its southerly end, is an important wetland nature reserve.

On the resort side 'Matko' was allowed to bring in the earth-movers and fell non-native trees to create a course of great natural beauty that opened in 1998. His design philosophy 'Listen to the land' is no different from Old Tom Morris's idea, but for the course at Arabella, he also had to listen to the developers. The 18 holes wind their way through long ribbons of discreet housing, not unlike Valderrama.

Most elegant of all is the 8th hole, a par-5 which sweeps downhill to a green on a small peninsula jutting out into the lagoon. Overshoot, and you'll be in amongst a wide variety of indigenous wildfowl. The 18th hole runs parallel to the lagoon edge, a fitting end to the round with a bunker at water's edge the entire length acting as a buffer, making it more likely that a wayward shot at the close will be from sand and not end up in the reed beds.

THE MAJLIS STARTED A REVOLUTION IN GOLF TOURISM. NOW IT'S 'THE OLD COURSE' OF THE MIDDLE EAST

Opposite top Cameron Young plays his second shot from sand on the 8th hole towards the glittering spires of Dubai.

Opposite bottom Rory McIlroy hits a long putt on the 18th green during the 2024 Hero Dubai Desert Classic.

Above The unique clubhouse of the Majlis Course during the first round of the 2024 Hero Dubai Desert Classic.

EMIRATES GOLF CLUB

DUBAI, UNITED ARAB EMIRATES

Bahrain might have got in early with the first Formula 1 race — soon followed by Abu Dhabi, Qatar and Saudi Arabia. But it was Sheikh Mohammed bin Rashid Al Maktoum who proposed the first 18-hole grass golf course in the Middle East.

American Karl Litten was responsible for bringing the Sheikh's vision to life and what seemed like a wealthy man's indulgence, the miracle Majlis course, opened for play in 1988. That was the start. Since the turn of the century there has been a boom in new courses in Dubai and the list of designers reads like a *Who's Who* of 1990s golf — Ernie Els, Nick Faldo, Colin Montgomerie, Ian Baker-Finch, Greg Norman, Thomas Bjørn are all involved.

However, the Majlis is the Old Course of Dubai. It's the venue for the Dubai Desert Classic tournament, with the classic image of players teeing off at the 8th hole with the glittering towers of the new metropolis beyond. The course

stretches out to 7,301 yards from the back tees with a par set at 72, playing through ribbons of green set amongst loose sand (little hardpan) and saltwater lakes. Ernie Els managed to make it round in 61 in 1994 and no-one's bettered that since.

And while St Andrews has its R&A Clubhouse, players on the Majlis repair to the Royal Pavilion styled in the fashion of a Bedouin tent. Many Bedouin tents. The second course at the Emirates Club was designed by Nick Faldo and started life in 1996 as a nine-holer, 'The Wadi' (the Arabic word for valley), after the wadi that runs the length of the course. A decade later and Nick extended it to a challenging 18 holes with the same jaw-dropping skyline as the Majlis, and the ability to play floodlit golf in the cool of the evening air. For golfers who don't like to travel too far out of town, the Emirates Club is the perfect destination.

GOLFERS MIGHT FEEL RELUCTANT TO TAKE A DIVOT OUT OF THESE EXQUISITELY PREPARED FAIRWAYS

HAESLEY NINE BRIDGES

HAESLEY, SOUTH KOREA

Everything looks under control at Haesley Nine Bridges — the fairway cut, the exemplary greens, the flow of the water from the lake, even some of the trees are restrained by hawsers. It looks monitored and manicured to within an inch of its perfect life.

It is a follow-on from the successful Nine Bridges course on Jeju Island and the creation of developer J.H. Lee. He drafted in the same design team, while also hiring the services of Marsh Benton, which may sound like the name of a village in the fens but is actually the name of Augusta National's Director of Agronomy. He advised on the installation of sub-air and hydronics systems for every green. The first system allows air to be injected into the soil under the putting surfaces, preventing a build-up of excess moisture, while the second keeps the greens at a stable temperature. They are thoroughly cosseted.

Haesley means 'the village with the rising sun' and despite its hilly location it's claimed that the sunrise can be seen from everywhere on the course. The immaculate condition of the 18 holes revealed by Gary Lisbon's detailed photography gives the impression that it is a short track, but it is a par-72 stretching to 7,265 yards from the back tees.

Opposite top The 6th hole is one of the more conventional layouts at Haesley with no sign of water or bridges...

Opposite bottom ...unlike the 7th with its green to the side of the small lake that feeds the waterfall, tumbling down by the first green.

Above The manicured fairway and approach to the 18th green. For those who dislike rough, there is little to be found on the course.

Left Everything about Haesley Nine Bridges is well thought out, including the halfway pavilion, the clubhouse and the 50's Futuristic starting booth.

There are generous forward tees, too, and many of the greens have extended front aprons which are almost indistinguishable from the cut of the green. Were the great golfing maverick, the pipe-smoking Brian Barnes still alive one could easily imagine him trying to take a putter off the tee (as he did in the 1965 Dutch Open) at the par-3, 15th.

That would be unlikely on the 1st hole, a dramatic opening to the round, it is a short par-4 to an island green below a waterfall tumbling over a rocky outcrop. Throughout the round the sound of falling water is rarely far away; the use of streams, ponds and waterfalls, though clearly contrived has assumed a high state of *feng shui*. Water comes into play on many holes but its use is almost always

ingenious and artful. The course opened in 2009 and it has bedded in nicely.

You will definitely find nine bridges on this course and no straight lines, other than in the similarly jaw-dropping clubhouse, a winner of World Architecture awards and the antithesis of the R&A's Victorian clubhouse. The contrast in courses is stark as well. Haesley is like a golf course inserted into one of the world's great Japanese gardens with everything neatly in place. It would be interesting to see the reaction of golfers only exposed to this most managed of courses to the wild, tussocky, hummocky dunes of Ballybunion or Machrihanish.

NICK FALDO'S PICTURE PERFECT VIETNAMESE COURSE HAS ENOUGH SAND TO RIVAL PINE VALLEY — AND A LOT MORE JUNGLE...

LAGUNA LĂNG CÔ

CÙ DÙ, VIETNAM

Vietnam is a country transformed from the war-ravaged throws of the late sixties and early seventies to a burgeoning tourist economy leaning heavily on golf. Cù Dù was once a small fishing village in central Vietnam on the long coastal strip overlooked by the Trường Sơn Mountains.

Today it is a vacation town and at the heart of it, Laguna Lăng Cô, a facility to match the best that Phuket in Thailand can offer. It's a 700-acre resort where golfers can stay and play, or live and play, close to a two-mile beach overlooking the East Sea. It's an area that is marketed as: 'Renowned for its pristine coastline, natural scenery and proximity to UNESCO World Heritage Sites.'

The Nick Faldo-designed course, No.26 in the timeline, is a beauty. It threads out and back in traditional manner through a tropical jungle, but with added elements you are unlikely to find on a first world course. Early in the round fairways pass by terraced paddy fields still traditionally cultivated by locals using water buffalo.

Faldo had a prodigious amount of sand to work with and while some fairways have the luxurious carpeted feel of a Hawaiian course, others have areas of sandy scrub that resemble the carries required at Pine Valley. Some of

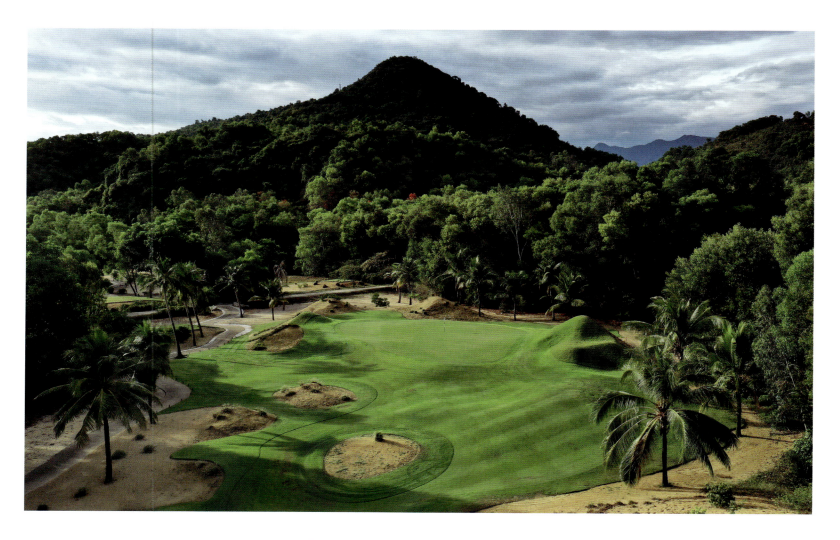

the fairways, such as the 11th, are lined by large, rounded sedimentary rocks with the same kind of hue as those found on Easter Island, giving the course added gravitas.

Star of the show is the par-3, 8th hole, straight out of the musical *South Pacific*. Although it only measures 162 yards from the back tee it is an island green in an ocean of sand with a small landing area and a wealth of contours to navigate on the putting surface. This is followed by the tree-fringed 9th, a par-4 which follows the edge of the beach to the far end of the property, sand lapping at the fairway all along. Laguna Lăng Cô is a course filled with character and though it can play to just under 7,100 yards and a par-71, the forward tees ensure that it can fulfil its mission to entertain.

ONE OF THE WORLD'S UNIQUE GOLF COURSES — AND THAT'S BEFORE THE INCLUSION OF THE 'EXTREME 19TH' WHICH REQUIRES A HELICOPTER

Above Impala and water buffalo roam across the 7th hole, designed by Colin Montgomerie.

Opposite top Despite having the whole of Africa to aim at, players struggle to hit the green at the Extreme 19th.

Opposite bottom Hanglip Mountain as viewed from the green of the Extreme 19th. The world's longest par-3.

LEGEND GOLF AND SAFARI RESORT
WATERBERG, LIMPOPO PROVINCE, SOUTH AFRICA

The Legend Golf and Safari Resort is a three-hour drive from Johannesburg in the 54,000 acres of the Entabeni Safari Conservancy. It has become famous for one hole, not encountered on its Signature golf course, the Extreme 19th played from a tee high up on Hanglip Mountain.

The Legends course is a monster 8,510 yards long from the championship tees, 7,887 yards from the professional tees and a titchy 7,375 yards for mere mortals, although with hard fairways and an altitude of around 2,000 feet, the ball will travel far.

Each of the 18 holes played across the *bushveld* landscape was designed by an illustrious golf professional — the likes of Bernhard Langer, Jim Furyk, Ian Woosnam, Colin Montgomerie, Thomas Bjørn, Justin Rose, Luke Donald, Padraig Harrington, Retief Goosen, Sergio Garcia, Vijay Singh and Trevor Immelman all put their name to a hole as

part of a bold marketing plan. Each tee features a map of the hole and information about its designer, so players can make their own judgement call as to whether their design skills outweigh their past ability from tee to green.

Once players have completed the par-5, 18th it's time for a helicopter ride from the luxurious Signature Clubhouse to the top of Hanglip Mountain.

At the Extreme 19th golfers are given the chance to hit six balls down to the Africa-shaped green located 470 yards below. A ball that lands inside the designated playing area, can then be played across the continent to the flagstick and the score is logged in the 'Hall of Fame'. It's an unreal experience, but then again playing golf in a set from *The Lion King* will certainly prepare golfers for the most iconic of extra holes.

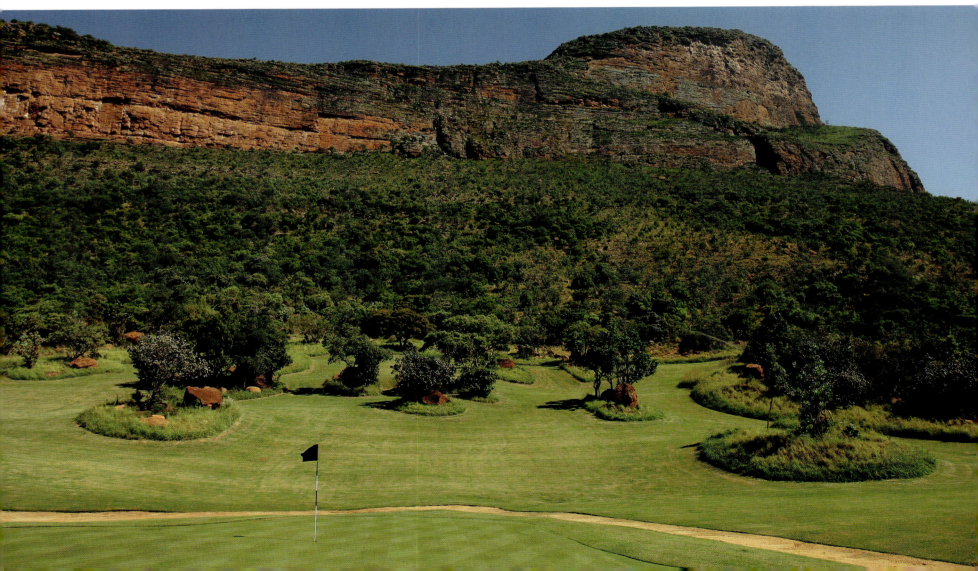

WITH A HANDFUL OF TOP COURSES ON THE BAJA CALIFORNIA PENINSULA, QUIVIRA TAKES ITS PLACE AS THE MOST SPECTACULAR

QUIVIRA

LOS CABOS, BAJA CALIFORNIA, MEXICO

Jack Nicklaus's golf course designs in Mexico have produced some stunning results. His first venture south of the border, the Arroyo and Mountain nine-hole courses at Palmilla, close to the tip of Baja California, were a formidable start in 1993. He also designed the famous 'Tale of the Whale' island hole at Punta Mita Pacifico. This is an 194-yard blow into the Pacific Ocean with a landing spot on a green transplanted to a triangular rocky island that from above looks like the tail of a whale. To find where your ball has ended you need to take a trip at low tide or use an amphibious vehicle.

At Quivira, Jack has created two even more spectacular par-3s with the 192-yard 6th hole and 144-yard 13th both defying gravity and clinging to a cliff face with golf-ball-hungry rocks below. And no specialist vehicles other than a golf cart are needed to access the greens.

To play at Quivira golfers need to book a stay at one of the Pueblo Bonito Resorts in Los Cabos. And while the Palmilla courses are close to the tip of the Baja peninsula, they look towards the Sea of Cortez. The course at Quivira

is on the very tip — and heading south, the next land you're going to hit is Easter Island.

Quivira is the centrepiece of what is an 1,850-acre luxury resort. Opened in 2014 it was eight years in the making. Given the nature of the infrastructure, the cart tracks, the irrigation and the inaccessibility, that's hardly surprising — the course is very spread out and carts are compulsory.

With that decision having been made, it has freed Jack up to lay out holes over tremendously different terrain. There are mountain holes and links-style holes all in the same round. It's one of the few courses where a satnav might come in handy. Starting low-down at sea level, there is a lengthy transition between the 4th green on the arroyo, or flat outwash, and the 5th tee way up on the cliffs. There are also reasonable excursions between the 13th green and 14th tee, and the 15th green and 16th tee, and it's best not to be a nervous passenger when the course takes to the cliff edge.

Given the heat that can be experienced on Mexican courses, the resort has installed three separate halfway houses at the 5th, 9th, and 16th holes. The outlook from the 9th 'cantina' is stupendous and worthy of a visit even if by that time a player has dumped all their balls onto the beach below the 5th and 6th holes. It may not be a course suitable for acrophobics, but for everyone else Quivira is an iconic course they must play.

HAMILTON ISLAND GOLF CLUB

KAURI CLIFFS

KINGSTON HEATH

TE ARAI

BARNBOUGLE

JACK'S POINT

CAPE KIDNAPPERS

AUSTRALIA AND NEW ZEALAND

HAVING STARTED OUT AS A MODERN
LINKS, BARNBOUGLE HAS NOW ADDED
COURSES TO BECOME A RESORT
DESTINATION

Opposite top The Dunes' closing hole.
The earlier course is a more traditional
out-and-back configuration than the
compact Lost Farm course.

Opposite bottom Tucker Creek
separates Barnbougle Dunes (left)
from Barnbougle Lost Farm (right).

Above The monster, 487-yard, par-4,
8th hole at Barnbougle Dunes.

BARNBOUGLE

BRIDPORT, TASMANIA, AUSTRALIA

Barnbougle Dunes and Barnbougle Lost Farm are modern
classics. Developed by Mike Keiser, the man behind Bandon
Dunes, the development has a similar *Field of Dreams* ethos
— if you build it, they will come. In this case a flight across
the Bass Straight from Melbourne — a bit more involved
than the five-hour drive from Portland, but the same idea.
Build a great course and golfers will beat a path to your door.

Keiser is a man totally invested in the joy of links golf
and naturally turned to his trusted Bandon confederates for
designs. Tom Doak, with help from Australian ex-pro Michael
Clayton, created the Dunes course (2004), and when that
success was confirmed, Coore & Crenshaw set to work on
Lost Farm (2010).

The plot of land on Tasmania's northeast coast had
previously been the seaward side of a potato farm. The
dune land is quite different either side of Tucker Creek. To
the west of the inlet, the Dunes course is more like the low,
grassy rolling sand dunes of Scotland. To the east the dunes

become steeper and more dramatic, like the classic monster
hillocks encountered on Ireland's west coast.

The Dunes has nine holes out and back to the west, and
then another nine holes out and back along a coastal strip
to the east. Lost Farm, being the other side of the creek,
has a separate clubhouse and meanders inland with six
greens fringing the shore and one up the creek. It also has
the luxury of 20 holes with a crafty 13a as a substitute hole,
should one of the regulars need maintenance, and 18a, a
short par-3, leading from the 18th green to right outside
the clubhouse bar — even though the walk back in is very
short indeed.

For those whose concentration lasts just ninety
minutes, there is now Bougle Run — a short course from Bill
Coore nestled between the higher dunes of Lost Farm and
consisting of 12 par-3s and two par-4s. No doubt we will
soon see a 36-hole putting course like St Andrews' famous
Himalayas (see Streamsong and Bandon Dunes).

ONE OF THE WORLD'S MOST RECOGNIZABLE GOLF COURSES RARELY FINDS ITSELF OVERPLAYED

CAPE KIDNAPPERS

TE AWANGA, HAWKE'S BAY, NEW ZEALAND

The brief note in the Hawke's Bay tourist guide says it all: 'Cape Kidnappers is a low-volume facility, playing approximately 30 rounds of golf per day.' It was the second of Julian Robertson's New Zealand ventures and matched his first, Kauri Cliffs, for spectacle and sheer golfing adventure. And exclusivity.

Hawke's Bay on the North Island is best known for its wine production and the glorious art deco architecture of Napier, a city almost wholly rebuilt in the 1930s after it was destroyed in a 1931 earthquake. At the southern tip there is Cape Kidnappers, named by James Cook in 1769 after a local Māori tribe attempted to abduct a member of his crew.

By the time he was asked to design the second course at Te Ārai, Tom Doak must have been well acquainted with the North Island. He was commissioned to design the course at Cape Kidnappers in the early millennium. The site he was given bordered towering cliffs, plunging 500 feet to the pounding Pacific below.

Almost all the holes follow a north-easterly slant, aligning with the Te Aute limestone ridges that divide up the ground. The front nine are very much inland, yet highly engaging. Those suffering vertigo can avoid any rise in blood pressure by doing two loops — although the 6th green does give an indication of what's in store after the turn.

The 10th then takes golfers out towards the ridges that have become the distinctive feature of the course, beloved by drone photographers. It is in the second half of the round that golfers go close to the edge, though on the ground, the fairways often aren't as intimidating as they look from above. From the 12th onwards it's all ridge play with a behemoth of a par-5, the 651-yard 15th hole that flows gently down to the

sea to a mercifully flat green. Then it's a quick peer over the edge of the 16th tee — if you dare — and back uphill again.

Two decades before he became the 'Torquemada' of Te Ārai, Doak was far more resort-minded with his green contours at Cape Kidnappers... though players *will* find an elephant buried on the 14th green. The final green is in a neat hollow by the unostentatious clubhouse, designed with a tin roof to fit in with the sheep-farming aesthetic of the locality. Inside, the décor is as elegant as one might expect from an expensive resort, and players can toast their success or drown their sorrows at great shots which somehow ended up in Hawke's Bay. If only they had some decent local wines to do it with...

Opposite top The coastline holes may get all the plaudits, but the inland ones are equally as challenging — here, the uphill 2nd.

Opposite bottom The par-3, 3rd hole requires a significant carry, in excess of 200 yards.

Top The 13th tee and green perched at the end of the land, before golfers mount the 14th tee above for a drive across the valley, then taking the footbridge to the 14th fairway.

Above left The view from the 18th tee — one final carry.

Above right Cape Kidnappers' clubhouse fits perfectly with the local architecture.

MANY OF THE HOLES RUN ALONG THE SPINE OF DENT ISLAND AND SO THE PANORAMIC VIEWS FROM THE COURSE ARE SUBLIME

HAMILTON ISLAND GOLF CLUB

DENT ISLAND, QUEENSLAND, AUSTRALIA

North of Brisbane, off the Queensland coast, there is a group of islands known as the Whitsundays, named after the passage that Captain James Cook sailed through on that day in June 1770. He would have passed close to Hamilton Island, today a busy tourist destination for those drawn by the sub-tropical climate and the chance to visit the Great Barrier Reef.

A short ferry ride from Hamilton Island is Dent Island which hosts a unique and challenging golf course. Opened in 2009, it was designed by five-time Open Champion Peter Thomson, one of his last course commissions, but unquestionably the most spectacular.

Though it bills itself as a championship course, the club reassures visitors at the same time that it is suitable for keen amateurs through to experienced professionals. This is a holiday destination, after all. Players have the choice of three tees marked out as: Hoop pine, Pandanas (or screwpine) and Grass tree. Hoop pine is the longest while Grass tree is the shortest.

There are two distinct nine-hole circuits — both of which return (eventually) to the central clubhouse and both give fabulous views to the rocky coves and beaches of other Whitsunday Islands. The first nine stick close to the clubhouse at the northern end, while the second nine stretch their legs and head south in glorious isolation to the tip of Dent Island, making the turn after the 15th green.

Thomson and his partner Ross Perrett clearly ran out of suitable terrain after the 17th green, because from there it's a couple of par-5s of walking distance — admittedly, through some tremendous scenery — to get to the 18th tee, but from there players get one of the truly great panoramas for a final hole.

Above A view looking over the short 4th hole to the ridge-running, par-5, 5th hole, which is followed by another par-5, the 6th.

Left A side view of the par-4, 15th green, at the furthest flung point on the course.

Opposite top After the par-3, 16th hole, the green of which is visible near the top of the hill, it's downhill to the 17th tees, and the 17th green at the bottom of the frame.

Opposite bottom It's a journey to get to the 18th tee, but the final hole — the fairway running right to left — doesn't disappoint.

Left Visiting players are obliged to continue their round after putting out on the 7th green, when the temptation might be to sit and take it all in.

WITH THE REMARKABLES MOUNTAIN RANGE AS A BACKDROP AND LAKE WAKATIPU BELOW, THIS IS A BREATHTAKING GOLF COURSE

JACK'S POINT

JACK'S POINT, QUEENSTOWN, NEW ZEALAND

Queenstown is the thrill-seeker's capital of New Zealand. Having given us bungee jumping and jet-boat rides, the rugged South Island has now produced a golf course to heighten the senses.

The country's most famous golfer, Bob Charles, partnered with John Darby to create Jack's Point, 18 holes that blend seamlessly with the natural grassy terrain of this barren, post-glaciated landscape.

Only 20 minutes outside of Queenstown, the course, which opened in 2008, is like playing golf in the wilder glens of Grampian Scotland where they meet the coastal waters of the Western Isles. Except the jagged peaks of the Remarkables mountain range far exceed the highest Munro summit and Lake Wakatipu is an ample substitute for the saltwater lochs. They are breathtaking backdrops, and at an elevation of more than 1,000 feet, some of that breath is already taken.

The course has been plotted through tussocky grassland with minimal earth moving, yet it still manages to incorporate infinity greens, on the 5th, 6th and 7th, three perfect vistas looking out onto the lake, with the putting surface easily fitting in with the naturalistic style, as though the ground was there ready and waiting.

The 8th hole is the last of the lakeside wonders, with commanding views down each of the U-shaped valleys that Lake Wakatipu fills.

Throughout the course there are small granite outcrops and sentinel rocks, and simple tee markers add to the rustic approach. The presence of golf buggies on the course may be necessary but they're jarring.

After the par-3, 11th, players turn and head inland with only the consolation of soaring mountain peaks for a view. These holes run through typical sheep-grazing land with dry stone boundary walls and the necessity to clear one on the 15th, a nice nod to the links at North Berwick.

It's a wholly different style to the other stand-out Kiwi courses and no less impressive. And unlike its other great rivals, players are not required to phone their bank manager before booking a tee time.

Top The uphill par-4, 4th hole with the backdrop of the Remarkables mountain range.

Above This side view of the 4th green gives the alternative view from that hole, and both are outstanding.

Opposite top The 197-yard, par-3, 13th hole with a big carry over native grassland.

Opposite bottom Three tees for the par-4, dogleg final hole, with the lake coming in to play for the most direct route to the green.

DAVID HARMAN'S EASY-ON-THE-EYE COURSE PRESENTS MANY CHALLENGES TO ITS EXCLUSIVE CLIENTELE.

Above **The par-4, 9th hole demands a drive up the 'Giant's Steps' to a hillside green.**

Opposite top **There are few options other than to go for it on the lengthy par-3, 7th hole, which can be 217 yards from the back tee.**

Opposite bottom **The 6th hole introduces a chasm into the range of landforms thrown at players.**

KAURI CLIFFS

TAKOU BAY, NORTH ISLAND, NEW ZEALAND

It was a bold move to create Kauri Cliffs. In the late 1990s Bandon Dunes was just a speck on the horizon and Tara Iti had not been conceived, yet American developer Julian Robertson stuck his neck out to create a resort golf course 170 miles north of Auckland. Although New Zealand, particularly the South Island around Dunedin, is said to be the Scotland of the Southern Hemisphere, golf has not been a major part of the nation's sporting life, let alone a high-end golfing destination. After Robertson bought a 4,500-acre sheep farm overlooking Takou Bay that was about to change.

He hired Jack Nicklaus protégé David Harman and handed over the map. Given that you can fit a championship level course inside 200 acres, the designer was spoiled for choice. Ultimately he chose a route that maximized the site's greatest asset, its unimpeachable views.

Having land to play with, he was also able to spread the 18 holes across hillsides — not exactly the Pine Valley approach, where George Crump had prescribed that each hole should be separate from the others, the site was too open for that — but the shout of 'Fore!' is not likely to be heard during a round.

It may be a resort course to look at, but there are still holes that are as tough as they are beautiful. Take the par-4 6th hole where players must drive across a chasm lined with a forest of native tree ferns. It's not a long hole, but in golf, deep carries have their own special gravity. Next up is the par-3, 7th, 200+ yards from the back tee where a ravine must be crossed and the natural slopes around the green are likely to send the ball tumbling downhill. That's if it is not already in one of the many bunkers surrounding the hole.

To round off the front nine there's an uphill par-4 known as 'Giant Steps' which demands another ravine drive onto a fairway with four prominent ledges or steps, before players can get their breath back in the clubhouse for a halfway stop.

The back nine are more like an out-and-back with the 'out' inland through valley and marshland which act as a counterpoint, before the 13th crests the hill and the views across to the Cavalli Islands are revealed once more. Given the green fees, the location and resort costs it's a once-in-lifetime experience. Or, make that two. After Kauri Cliffs there's the sister venue at Cape Kidnappers, 500 miles to the south.

Right Shorter than it looks, the exquisite par-4, 16th hole is little more than 350 yards long, but an accurate approach is required.

VYING WITH ROYAL MELBOURNE
AS AUSTRALIA'S BEST SANDBELT
COURSE — BOTH HAVE THAT ALISTER
MACKENZIE TOUCH

Opposite top Photographer Gary
Lisbon is an early riser, as evidenced
by this balloon shot from behind the
carefully contoured 10th green.

Opposite bottom An aerial view of the
short, par-3, 15th green.

Above The 460-yard, par-4, 6th hole
returns to the clubhouse. The first tee
is to the right of frame.

KINGSTON HEATH

MELBOURNE, VICTORIA, AUSTRALIA

The Sandbelt region in the southeast suburbs of Melbourne is rich in golf courses. Kingston Heath is emblematic of this high density of top clubs, similar in approach to its better-known neighbour Royal Melbourne, but edging it out in terms of player reviews.

The club was formed in 1909 and laid out in a tight parcel of land by Australian architect Dan Soutar. Despite the confines he managed to create a course of 6,800 yards, something very much admired by Alister MacKenzie when he came to advise on installing bunkers in 1926.

MacKenzie had been commissioned by Royal Melbourne to design their West Course, but having made the long trip to Australia, he picked up a £250 fee for adding suitable hazards around Kingston Heath. It would be interesting to know if the course gave him ideas for the Worcester Golf Club at Broughton Park which he went on to design a year later, on an equally compact parcel of ground.

Over time, non-native trees and inappropriate native trees, such as the Mahogany gum, were added and in the decades when little was spoken of the heritage of golf courses, many of the MacKenzie bunkers were filled in.

In 1982 this neglect of the past was halted by newly appointed course superintendent Graeme Grant, who hauled out maps and photos from 1937 and showed members how many of the 18 holes had strayed from Soutar and MacKenzie's originals. Bunkers were duly rebuilt and gum trees removed. It helped his cause that he was restoring the work of a man who had guided the creation of Augusta National and Cypress Point.

Today, Kingston Heath is not just another Sandbelt course in the Melbourne suburbs, it is a toss of the coin as to whether it's the best in Australia. In many ways that is thanks to a diligent member in the 1930s who went round photographing every hole.

Above The 2nd hole on the North Course is a 250-yard, par-3 which will require a strong accurate blow to get on the putting surface.

Opposite top The 11th fairway on the North Course runs parallel with the 8th which heads in the opposite direction.

Opposite bottom Looking back from behind the par-4, 7th green on the North Course.

TE ĀRAI

TE ĀRAI, NORTH ISLAND, NEW ZEALAND

The local Māori meaning of Te Ārai is 'the other side of the veil'. The other side of New Zealand's impressive Tara Iti golf links is Te Ārai, a brace of courses to be found 90 minutes' drive from the capital Auckland.

Tom Doak had designed the instantly acknowledged Tara Iti links on pristine coastal land without the need for widescale bulldozing of dune complexes. It has since become a private club. The developer, Ric Kayne, decided to make use of a further coastal strip, just to the south, bordering on one of North Auckland's great white sand surfing beaches. The intention was to cash in on demand created by the allure of Tara Iti, but like the movie *Godfather II*, the follow-up has exceeded the original.

Coore and Crenshaw were slated to get first choice on the site and when they arrived they found a forest at the edge of the ocean. This was commercial forestry, though, planted in the mid-twentieth century, not treasured rain forest that cloaks a lot of New Zealand. It could go. Beneath was sandy terrain, perfect for a links course. Bill and Ben started up the chainsaw.

Their South Course starts into the trees for the first three holes before emerging into open links land for one of the longest stretches of beachside holes to be found on a modern links course. Turn the corner at the 5th green and as Gary Lisbon's immaculate course photography shows, the view down the 6th hole fairway presents a stunning vista of the holes ahead. The fairways are broad, yet without the devious, rage-inducing slants of an old links course, and with few carries and little rough, players might face the startling prospect of finishing a round with the same ball that they started with.

Tom Doak's North Course opened in 2023 and it allows Te Ārai's owners to rotate access with members and visitors. One day, the South Course will be open to visitors, but the North restricted to members only. The following day it reverses, thus allowing those who want to stay and play, the chance to experience both.

Doak's North Course is viewed as tougher than the South, routing more inland, though with four holes at the ocean's edge — the opening two and the closing two.

There's a distinct difference between the two courses despite their proximity. Whereas the South is open and wind-blown, the mature trees frame the expansive fairways of the North — at times the course is swallowed up by the forest, only to re-emerge with a view of the coast through lonesome strands of pine. And everywhere sand.

What distinguishes both courses is the ingenious complexity of some of the greens, particularly on the North Course where Doak relished the opportunity of employing knolls, tiers, strange borrows and cambers in a dazzling array of curves that delight the eye, but punish the scoring. The fairways might be wide, the bounce true, the rough light, but the flagsticks can be elusive.

With the South only opening in 2022 and the North a year later, these two courses will soften and mature from the prodigies they are. It might be an idea to play them before they, too, become private like Tara Iti.

Above Te Ārai's South Course features more holes running by the coast than the North. The closing four holes of the front nine, and the final four of the back nine all hug the shoreline.

Opposite top The short par-4, 6th hole on the South Course has a cavernous bunker that simply begs big hitters to take it on.

Opposite bottom The par-3, 8th green on the South Course.

INDEX